M000210918

FLYING STAR FENG SHUI
FOR PERIOD 8

BY LILLIAN TOO

FLYING STAR FENG SHUI
For **PERIOD 8**

Which Starts Feb 4th 2004

Enhancing wealth, health & relationship
luck for the next twenty years

LILLIAN TOO

KONSEP BOOKS
KONSEP LAGENDA SDN BHD (223 855)
Kuala Lumpur 59100 MALAYSIA

WEBSITES:
www.lillian-too.com
www.wofs.com
Email: ltoo@wofs.com

LILLIAN TOO'S
FLYING STAR FENG SHUI FOR PERIOD 8
© Konsep Lagenda Sdn Bhd

ISBN **983 9778-76-5**
This edition first published in Malaysia in
August 2003

Reprint December 2003

2nd Reprint January 2004

This book is dedicated to
Jennifer
and her team at
World of Feng Shui.
May they enjoy
great good fortune
all through the
Period of Eight.

OTHER BOOKS BY LILLIAN TOO

Published by
KONSEP BOOKS
The Goddess Oracle
The ABC of Feng Shui
Eight Mansions Feng Shui
Flying Star Feng Shui
Practical Applications of Feng Shui
Water Feng Shui for Wealth
Dragon Magic - My Feng Shui Stories
Feng Shui Symbols of Good Fortune
Chinese Astrology for Romance & Relationships
Basic Feng Shui
Personalized Feng Shui Tips
The Chinese Dragon
Strategies for Career Success
Creative Visualization
Tap the Power Inside You
Explore the Frontiers of Your Mind
Feng Shui Gems – Love
Feng Shui Gems – Wealth
Feng Shui Gems – Children
Feng Shui Gems – Millenium
Feng Shui Gems – Career

Published by
**ELEMENT, AN IMPRINT OF
HARPERCOLLINS**PUBLISHERS
Lillian Too's Flying Star Feng Shui for the Master Practitioner
Smart Feng Shui for the Home
Irresistable Feng Shui Magic
Feng Shui Year 2002
The Complete Illustrated Guide to Feng Shui
The Complete Illustrated Guide to Feng Shui for Gardeners
The Fundamentals of Feng Shui
Feng Shui in Eight Easy lessons

Published by
**RIDER, AN IMPRINT OF EBURY PRESS,
RANDOM HOUSE**

Published by
COLLINS and BROWN

Published by
CICO BOOKS UK

CONTENTS

INTRODUCTION

My dear readers,

Feng shui is a living skill that promises tantalizing benefits to those who know how to use it correctly. But you will find that its potency is enhanced when **time** calculations are incorporated in to spatial concepts. There is thus a **space** as well as a **time** dimension to feng shui. And as your understanding of it increases, you will discover that there is an element of the scientific in its practice, and that it requires the use of a reliable compass.

Today, as acceptance of feng shui grows worldwide, it has become very popular with the West and with a new generation of overseas Chinese. As its popularity grows, more of its secrets are being revealed to the English-speaking world. Complex aspects of the practice, which had previously seemed challenging, are now eagerly sought.

Powerful compass formulas contained in my books on **Eight Mansions Feng Shui** and **Flying Star Feng Shui** add substantially to a fuller understanding of a complete feng shui practice. Secrets of Taoist feng shui practice, which use powerful mental consciousness techniques, are also becoming amalgamated into the broad based application of feng shui.

All this leads to a very comprehensive approach. Thus

while forms, shapes and symbols in the environment offer powerful inputs into the practice of space feng shui, today, the influence of rituals, mental consciousness, as well as time influences on one's luck, are gaining credence.

This book is about the dimension of time - how the mere passage of time alone can change the quality of Chi energy in homes and buildings. When you incorporate this dimension of feng shui into your practice, you will discover that the protection of your good fortune luck becomes immediately more complete.

TIME PERIOD FENG SHUI

Feng shui luck transformations over time are analysed using feng shui formulas that deal with time periods. These formulas are collectively referred to as **Flying Star Feng Shui** formulas.

Flying Star feng shui is about understanding **numerology** - i.e. the meanings of numbers and their combinations. Calculations are required, but these are easy to learn. The essence of Flying Star feng shui is the diagnosis of any space based on numbers that are placed in a three-by-three sector grid known as the Lo Shu Square, according to a set formula or sequence. This square is usually referred to as the **natal chart** or the **period chart** of houses and buildings.

The natal chart is constructed using two sets of information as follows:

1. The year and period when the building was built or last renovated. There is controversy surrounding the definition of completion date and renovations. Not all masters use the same definition, especially on what constitutes a renovation. However most are agreed that **as long as the heaven and earth chi of any building are re energised** it counts as a renovation. The date when the renovation is done is what determines the period of the building.

2. The exact compass direction, which the building faces. In flying star feng shui, the 360 degrees of the compass is divided into 24 directions. These are referred to as the 24 mountains. In Chinese books on Flying Star feng shui, these 24 directions are given generic names. To simplify these directions, I refer to them simply as directions, 1, 2 or 3. Thus each of the eight compass directions are subdivided into three sub directions, thereby making 24 directions (8 multiplied by 3). So I refer to the 24 mountains as South 1, South 2 and South 3 and so forth.

There is controversy surrounding the definition of the **facing direction of buildings.** This confusion arises when it comes to determining which chart correctly applies to any home or building. You should examine these controversial issues before deciding which Period 7 and Period 8 chart best applies to your house.

FLYING STAR FENG SHUI

Flying Star feng shui does not just reveal the map luck of your home - it also offers information on the way luck changes from year to year. This annual updating of feng shui, however, must take place within the bigger picture of the period map luck of the house. So when you feng shui your house to ensure a good future, you must regard it as a dynamic practice that requires constant and regular updating. Chi energy is always changing, so you must study how these changes affect your luck at all times.

In Feb 2004, a very significant milestone in Flying Star feng shui takes place, because that is when **Period 7** ends and the next **Period 8** begins. **This takes place on February 4th 2004.**

This change has tremendous implications on the luck transformations of all buildings, and the change of luck will affect these buildings for twenty years. This book will walk you through the different things you can do to take advantage of this period change to capture great good luck for the next twenty years.

THE HSIA CALENDAR

The calendar used in this book is referred to as the HSIA or Chinese solar calendar. It is different from

the lunar calendar, which starts on a different day each year. The HSIA calendar begins its year on the equivalent of either February 4th or 5th of the Gregorian calendar.

The HSIA calendar is used when analySing the time influence on feng shui. Each HSIA year and month has a **ruling Lo Shu number** and thus a ruling Lo Shu square. It is the numbers and their sequential placement in this square that is the basis of time dimension feng shui.

HOW TO USE THIS BOOK

This book offers information on the luck of the eight sectors of any home for the homes considered period 7 and period 8 houses. Under the whole Flying Star system, there are a total of 144 different natal charts of houses based on 9 periods making up a full cycle. Each period is named after its ruling number, and each period has 16 categories of houses. Each period lasts 20 years.

So, for every period, there are sixteen different houses. It is the same for the period of 7 and for the new period of 8. In each period, houses are differentiated according to their **facing directions**. There are sixteen categories of directions, and thus 16 different Flying Star charts for each period.

The Flying Star charts of buildings (and houses) built or renovated between February 4th 1984 until February 4th 2004 are Period of 7 charts. For these houses, the same charts will continue to apply to the luck distribution of their homes **unless** they change their houses into period 8 houses. Whether or not you change the period of your house, and if you decide to do so, *how* one goes about changing the period of one's house forms the major raison d'etre of this book.

It might be useful to know at this stage that in Period of 8, the number 7, which was lucky all through period 7, becomes very unlucky. Meanwhile 8, already a very lucky number, will become an even luckier number from 2004 onwards. This will hold true for twenty years.

It is therefore important to look at the natal chart of your house and make an analysis of it with a view to perhaps changing your house to period 8.

In addition, you would also want to identify the danger sectors of your house at the start of each new year, and if you have the need to do so, even examine the luck changes from month to month. Time feng shui offers you the tools to undertake this analysis.

Please note that all branches of Chinese healing and luck enhancing practices believe in the tenet "prevention is infinitely better than cure".

As such the motivation behind this book is to show you how you are able to identify the sectors of your house that are afflicted each year. You should identify these sectors and take remedial and preventive measures, thereby saving yourself from the unnecessary aggravations of falling ill, losing a loved one, getting burgled, encountering an accident and even suffering substantial financial losses.

FENG SHUI ANNUAL AFFLICTIONS

When you know which sectors of your home or office are afflicted in each period, you can design your house to ensure good fortune all through the twenty years of a period. And when you are able to identify the afflictions of each year and month, you can take steps to install "cures" to overcome bad annual and month stars. The annual and month stars must be treated with respect, since any misfortunes caused by them is usually severe.

In addition, you must also note the taboos relating to renovations, shifting house and generally disturbing the energy of certain sectors of your house each year. In every New Year, there are different sectors to note where their Chi cannot be disturbed by digging, banging or knocking.

These are identified as the three palaces and they are:

- The palace of the Grand Duke Jupiter (in Chinese known as the **tai sui**)
- The palace of the Three Killings (in Chinese known as the **sarm saat**)
- The palace of the Five Yellow (in Chinese known as the **wu wang**)

Always note where these palaces are located each new year. They move and change places from year to year.

It is easy to cause misfortune to occur if one is unaware of the taboos to observe, since they override the good feng shui of your home when broken. Ignoring the annual flying star afflictions usually results in loss, accidents, illness, mishaps and a great deal of bad luck without you knowing why.

The year 2004 is the year of the monkey, and the year's annual chart is also the original Lo Shu square with the number 5 in the center. Preliminary indications suggest it is a challenging year. This year marks the end of the 7 period and the start of the 8 period, so it is a year of transition where we see the rise to prominence and power of new factions, new leaders and new ideas.

Period 8 will be less materialistic than Period 7 - we will see the coming of a new generation of icons and role models who symbolize the pursuit of knowledge over the pursuit of wealth. In good feng shui practice, it is

beneficial to go with the flow of the times. Nevertheless, it is just as important to put the remedies in place that are needed to combat a new batch of afflictions. Likewise, it is equally important to place feng shui enhancers to activate the new locations of good fortune stars. It is this dynamic approach that will ensure good feng shui for our future.

This book explains all the intangible forces that will be at work all through the period of 8 – the twenty years that stretch from February 4th 2004 to February 4th 2024. Many things will happen on the world stage during the next twenty years - but as long as you safeguard the Chi of your homes and work places, feng shui will help you survive and thrive through the next twenty years.

Feng shui is a wonderful practice that is neither religious nor spiritual. But practicing feng shui with a good heart and with a genuine kind motivation really does make it more potent and powerful. Look on feng shui as a living skill and you will begin to enjoy it without being obsessed by it.

With this book you should be able to diagnose the modifications required for your house because of the period change. If you are uncertain of your analysis you can always email me or wofs staff at **questions@wofs.com** .

Do not let **wannabbee** feng shui experts confuse you.

When in doubt, judge according to what you see. Remember that if a feng shui expert cannot help himself or herself, there is really no way he/she can help you. Feng shui is a very easy skill to learn, but less easy to master. It requires patience and careful analysis. This is why I always encourage people to "do your own feng shui". The level of commitment and care one expends on one's own feng shui is always a great deal more concerted than any feng shui consultant can offer.

This motivation lies behind my books – to inspire you to "do it yourself". Let feng shui help to enhance your life, bring you greater happiness and surprise you with its wonderful potency…

Kuala Lumpur, Malaysia
August 2003

Time
Dimension
Feng Shui

Chapter 1

Time Dimension in Feng Shui

There is a time dimension in feng shui that can work in tandem with or in conflict to the way our spaces have been designed. In addition to taking the energy of **space** into consideration, we must also examine the energy exerted by the passage of **time**. This must never be overlooked. Everyone's feng shui require regular updates, and this can be done in time frames of 20 years, of a single year or as months, weeks and even days. This is because **time Chi** changes all the time.

Time never stands still. Energy changes every moment, each minute and every hour, each day and every month. This is the essence of **yang chi** in the universal complementarity of **yin** and **yang** that lies at the heart of feng shui practice. To measure time, the Chinese devised the calendar, both a lunar as well as a solar calendar. In time dimension feng shui, we use the solar calendar to measure time, and this is also referred to as the **Hsia** calendar.

Time feng shui is very potent and powerful. It cannot be ignored. It must be factored into anyone's practice of this living skill. In the old days, the practice of time feng shui was a closely guarded secret used by learned Masters and passed on only to favoured disciples. These master practitioners would update the feng shui of their special clients each year to take account of the annual changes of Chi energy, as well as every twenty years, to take account of changes in period Chi that

occur every twenty years.

Updating one's feng shui every year, as well as at every **change of period**, requires additional inputs from the feng shui practitioner. In the old days, recommendations were made without explanations being given, so that a kind of mysticism came to be associated with the practice of feng shui. This was because time changes in feng shui were so potent and powerful that its effect would manifest quickly, thus bringing fame and fortune to the master consultant. Some of them came to be regarded as having **special powers**, able to transform luck as if by magic.

Today, many of the important "secrets" of Flying Star feng shui and its annual and period updates are available to anyone wishing to master this compass school formula. In understanding the formula and the basis on which the feng shui charts of houses for different years and periods are created, we have come to see feng shui in a more "scientific and dynamic light". Certainly not as magic!

This is good news, because it takes a great deal of the mystery out of feng shui practice. It also leaves less room for guesswork and encourages more people to have confidence in the practice. It benefits to take a scientific approach viewing feng shui as a skill, that can be learned, rather than as a metaphysical practice. I discovered that this is the best way to practice feng shui – viewing it as a living skill.

Although based on an ancient wisdom, it is nevertheless a technical subject requiring accuracy and regular practice to develop expertise. Flying Star feng shui uses specific formulas to determine the **luck map** of each time period and it prescribes cures or enhancers based on what the luck map reveals.

Types of Good Fortune and Misfortune

Good fortune and misfortune in feng shui is categorised according to how luck manifests and in accordance with its intensity. Luck can be divided into **three levels of intensities**, which can be either positive or negative, and into **four different manifestations** of either good fortune or misfortune.

Manifestations of positive **money or prosperity luck** can mean either the luck that brings wealth creation or it can mean higher income levels. The latter is generally associated with career luck, while the former with business and entrepreneurial luck.

Then there is the **good health luck**, which means having no problems with diseases and other physical ailments. Good health luck also extends into longevity luck and good descendents luck. This is a vitally important aspect of good fortune. Illness usually indicates a weakness of Chi and the prevalence of yin energies.

The third type of good luck is **relationship luck**, which covers the broad spectrum of family, love, marriage and the luck of having good employees. It covers all aspects of our interpersonal interactions with friends, colleagues and business associates. Feng shui recognises that having good relationship luck is the key to happiness, harmony and success.

Finally, the fourth type of luck is the **luck of personal growth and development.**

26

This means having the good fortune to be able to learn, make progress, as well as grow in mind and spirit. In many ways, this is the best kind of good fortune, for it means that we have the good fortune to expand our individual horizons, and to reach our own private highs and aspirations.

There are different methods for accessing each of these different types of good luck under the different compass formulas. Many of these methods have already been covered in my other books. However, it is a good reminder to clarify exactly what luck means and how it manifests. Understanding the nature of luck and identifying the kind of luck we want from our feng shui practice will make it easier to decide on the options that face us.

In addition to different types of luck, feng shui also distinguishes between three intensities of good or bad luck. Thus good luck can come as growth luck, ripening luck or as already blossomed luck.

Of the three, growth luck or **sheng chi** is the most desired because it spells the start of one's good fortune period. When one's good fortune is just starting to grow, it means we are at the start of a good cycle. Ripening luck is like the blossoming of good fortune, while good fortune that has already blossomed could suggest one is at the tail end of one's good fortune.

At this tail end stage, it is vital to know how to revitalize the Chi – give it a boost! Negative luck or misfortune also has three intensities. Mild bad luck is easier to bear as it simply suggests **weakening Chi**. There is **stagnant** or **dead Chi**, which brings illness, and finally there is **killing Chi**, which brings disasters and total loss.

Luck Sectors and Periods of Time

Feng shui practice enables you to identify the luck of sectors in any home at different periods of time, and these are defined in terms of compass direction sectors, which are summarised in a feng shui chart. There are altogether nine such sectors in any chart, and these are usually referred to as the **nine palaces** of a building. The luck sectors of the nine palaces change and bring different types of luck of different intensities in different time periods.

Periods of time are based on the numbers 1 to 9, so there are altogether nine periods of time. Each of these periods is said to last twenty years, so a complete cycle of time lasts 180 years. Each period is named after its ruling number and the luck of different sectors change with every change of period.

Knowing how to identify the sectors of good luck becomes the essence of Flying Star feng shui practice. More than that, a master practitioner is someone who is able to analyse all the numbers of the chart so that he/she is able to explain the nuances of different manifestations of luck as well as the intensities of the good fortune or misfortune.

In addition, the master practitioner is able to offer remedies and cures to overcome feng shui afflictions caused by the time changes in each of the sectors. Many of the cures use powerful symbols that are related to the element Chi of each of the sectors. Thus, when practising flying star feng shui, a good

knowledge of the symbols of good fortune, as well as the five elements, is a huge advantage.

No one can ignore the effects of time on the luck of their living and work space. The impact of time Chi on the luck of each of the sectors is usually very powerful. This is why it is so important to take note of the annual changes in the way the Chi flows and how these affect the distribution of good and bad luck energy in your house.

The annual changes of Chi are mapped out in what is referred to as the annual feng shui chart. It is this annual chart that shows you if your bedroom is afflicted by the presence of the illness or loss star numbers or whether your main door benefits from lucky star numbers. Those wanting to know more about the annual and monthly charts should refer to my books *Feng Shui For Interiors* and *Flying Star Feng Shui for the Master Practitioner*.

But probably more important than taking note of annual changes in Chi is also the need to update your feng shui when the twenty-year Chi energy changes.

This is called a PERIOD change and we are coming to a period change very soon.

This will happen on **February 4th 2004** when the current Period 7, which began in 1984, comes to an end. On February 4th 2004, we will enter into the **Period of 8**, and then totally fresh new Chi energy will flow into all the buildings of the world. This new Chi distribution will last until 2024 - a period of 20 years. Every keen feng shui practitioner MUST take this change into account.

February 2004

S	M	T	W	T	F	S
1	2	3	(4)	5	6	7
8	9	10	11	12	13	14
15	16	17	18	19	20	21
22	23	24	25	26	27	28
29

Period Change & Other Feng Shui Methods

It is important to understand that the effect on your luck caused by the period change is every bit as important as that caused by the buildings and roads around you and by the direction and placements of your furniture in each room inside the house. The influence of **time and space** Chi on the quality of one's feng shui have equal weight, and no feng shui analysis of any home or office can be complete without taking **both** types of Chi into consideration.

Practising time feng shui and period feng shui requires a working knowledge of **Flying Star Feng Shui**. I regard this as the more technical branch of feng shui. Flying Star feng shui is very potent, but it is also much easier to practise than other schools of feng shui, since it is very exact and clear-cut. A great deal of the judgmental guesswork is factored out of the practice of Flying Star feng shui. This is probably the greatest advantage of this method. When you undertake the analysis, and then make the necessary

changes correctly, the effects are felt very quickly. It is for this reason that all the feng shui currently practised in Hong Kong and Taiwan contain major inputs of this method.

But Flying Star feng shui formulas cannot be used in isolation.

You should not use Flying Star and ignore all other dimensions of feng shui, especially those aspects that deal with the celestial guardians – the dragon, tiger, phoenix and tortoise. And especially, you cannot ignore the

symbolic dimensions of feng shui. Indeed, almost all the afflictions identified under Flying Star feng shui and revealed through the natal charts generated under this method, use the strategic placement of different symbols as cures and remedies.

These symbols can be of the celestial animals of legends, or of powerful Taoist deities that personify wealth, health or longevity. Symbols can also be of fruits, plants and so forth. There are many different symbols of protection and symbols of good fortune. But it is the correct positioning of such symbols that enable us to overcome the afflictions of negative feng shui caused by changes of time.

Placement of symbols can also activate or energise the different types of **sheng chi** and other types of Chi, which reside in different corners of the home.

This book focuses specifically on the feng shui implications of the forthcoming period change. But you must remember at all times never to ignore other aspects of feng shui defined under other methods. This means that you must continue to observe everything you already know about feng shui that addresses its space dimensions.

Thus, when looking at the layout of rooms, the arrangement of furniture and the flow of Chi, the importance of shapes and of the environmental influences of Form School feng shui must be taken note of. In the excitement of learning Flying Star feng shui, it is so important that we do not forget all the other "rules" and "taboos" of feng shui. It is just that to get the most out of feng shui practice, we should also take into account the implications of time and period changes in feng shui.

The Ending of the Period of Seven

Time dimension feng shui divides time into 20-year periods with each period being ruled by a number. Since there are nine numbers 1 to 9, there are altogether nine periods that make up a complete cycle. Since each period lasts 20 years the complete cycle is 180 years. We are now at the tail end of the Period of 7, which began on February 4th 1984.
It comes to an end on February 4th 2004 when the Period of 8 takes over.

All through the past 20 years, when Period 7 reigned supreme, the number 7 was very lucky. As a result, many of the Period of 7 charts which contained the powerfully potent and auspicious **double 7** in the sector that contained the main front door brought wealth creation to those fortunate enough to benefit from these charts. They enjoyed what is referred to in feng shui as having the **double period star in the facing palace**.

Those of you who are living in houses that face South, Southwest, Northeast and North would have benefited enormously from this feature if the double 7 in your house had been properly activated. Merely having a frequently used door in such a sector would have activated the double 7.

However, since the number 7 reverts to its evil nature when the period changes to the

Period of 8, those of you who benefited from the 7's good fortune must now seriously consider changing your house into a period of 8 house. This is because the 7 brings robbery, loss, bloodshed and even violence during the period of 8.

If you cannot change the period of your house (if you see later sections, you will realise that changing the period of your house is not a simple matter) you must use cures and remedies to contain the negative impact of the now **very unlucky 7**.

The period of 7 was also a period when the West direction represented the "**direct spirit**" of the period. This caused the element of "small metal" to become very significant. The period thus saw major expansion in high-technology electronic devices (small metal is the element of the West).

Period 7 also heralded the start of the digital age, and this has forever changed the technology of communications.

Period 7 was also an age dominated by the West. California was thus one of the main engines of growth in the period of 7 (note the spectacular emergence of Internet and computer billionaires from California). In fact, computer technology has forever changed the way the world works. Period 7 thus saw the rise in importance and power of communication.

It was also a period when women benefited greatly from good fortune luck. They enjoyed success and recognition in almost every field of endeavour. This is because the Period of 7 is represented by the trigram **TUI**, which is a female trigram. In the new period, this will change.

What to Expect in Period of Eight

With period 7 now on the wane, we will see a different set of influences coming into play. While the rise in influence of women was a major feature of the Period of 7, especially in the West, the coming Period of 8 will see young men dominating the world's political, economic, and business stage. This is because the number 8 is symbolised by the trigram **KEN**, which represents the young man.

Period 8 will see the rise in influence of countries and provinces that lie to the Northeast of any land mass, because the direction that corresponds to 8 is the Northeast. In Asia, this signifies the rise in global influence of China, and perhaps also the two Koreas.

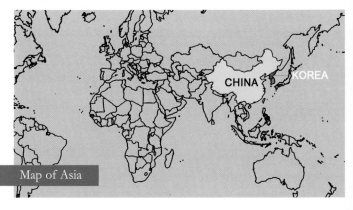

Map of Asia

In the United States, the NE direction points to the influence of New York, Washington and Boston. Where California was the main engine of growth in the period of 7, during the period of 8 we will see the Northeastern states taking a more pre-eminent role.

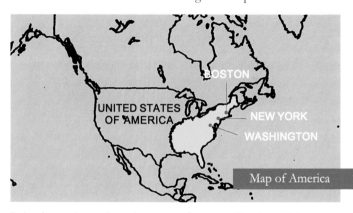

Map of America

It is also a time when the **mountain star** will reign. This means that health and relationships will exert far greater influences than money and wealth creation. The period of 7 stood for the lake, which signifies the water star's influence. This means that wealth creation was a prominent feature of the previous period. In the new period, the trigram **KEN** rules, and it stands for the mountain, which in turn suggests quiet strength and hidden treasures. This then will be the defining essence of the Period of 8. Yet the number 8 is also the luckiest of the nine numbers. In Chinese numerology, 8 is the luckiest of the **earth star numbers (2, 5 and 8)** and the luckiest of the **three white star numbers (1, 6 and 8)**. So those who make a special effort to tap into its potency will definitely attract extra good fortune.

In the coming period of 8 therefore, note the following:

- Those with KUA number 8 are in for an especially lucky period. Please refer to my book *Basic Feng Shui* to read about KUA numbers.

- Those with telephone numbers, car numbers and house numbers ending with 8, your luck sure has arrived!

- Those wearing or displaying the powerful **infinity** symbol, which is in reality the number 8 lying down, will enjoy extra good fortune.

Infinity sign

Those wearing or displaying the even more powerful **mystic knot** symbol will have the influence of the number tripled. If you examine the mystic knot closely, it is actually the infinity sign done three times. The mystic knot, carved out of jadeite, is shown here. Tying it with red thread activates its yang energy thereby making its properties come alive. For those who so wish, they can also wear the mystic knot in real gold and decorated with diamonds. This enhances the "earth" energy of the symbol, thereby making it far more potent.

Mystic knot

Find your Kua Number from the table below. Once you have your Kua Number, find your auspicious and inauspicious directions using the table on the right.

KUA NUMBERS AND YOUR DIRECTIONS

Your Kua #	Auspicious Direction	Inauspicious Direction
1	Southeast, East, South, North.	West, Northeast, Northwest, Southwest.
2	Northeast, West, Northwest, Southwest.	East, Southeast, South, North.
3	South, North, Southeast, East.	Southwest, Northwest, Northeast, West.
4	North, South, East, Southeast.	Northwest, Southwest, West, Northeast.
5	Northeast, West, Northwest, Southwest.	East, Southeast, South, North.
5	Southwest, Northwest, West, Northeast.	South, North, East, Southeast.
6	West, Northeast, Southwest, Northwest.	Southeast, East, North, South.
7	Northwest, Southwest, Northeast, West.	North, South, Southeast, East.
8	Southwest, Northwest, West, Northeast.	South, North, East, Southeast.
9	East, Southeast, North, South.	Northeast, West, Southwest, Northwest.

Birth Year	Kua # Male	Kua # Female
1910, 1919, 1928, 1937, 1946, 1955, 1964, 1973, 1982, 1991, 2000	9	6
1911, 1920, 1929, 1938, 1947, 1956, 1965, 1974, 1983, 1992, 2001	8	7
1912, 1921, 1930, 1939, 1948, 1957, 1966, 1975, 1984, 1993, 2002	7	8
1913, 1922, 1931, 1940, 1949, 1958, 1967, 1976, 1985, 1994, 2003	6	9
1914, 1923, 1932, 1941, 1950, 1959, 1968, 1977, 1986, 1995, 2004	5	1
1915, 1924, 1933, 1942, 1951, 1960, 1969, 1978, 1987, 1996, 2005	4	2
1916, 1925, 1934, 1943, 1952, 1961, 1970, 1979, 1988, 1997, 2006	3	3
1917, 1926, 1935, 1944, 1953, 1962, 1971, 1980, 1989, 1998, 2007	2	4
1918, 1927, 1936, 1945, 1954, 1963, 1972, 1981, 1990, 1999, 2008	1	5

Feng Shui Implications of the Forthcoming Period Change

The most important thing to remember in terms of feng shui is that as soon as the period changes, all Period 7 houses will immediately and instantly lose vitality and lose Chi strength. This means that for most of us who live in Period 7 houses, we will experience a loss in the vitality of our homes. Office buildings built in the period of 7 will likewise suffer the same weakening of Chi.

T his means that all houses, buildings, offices and apartments built or renovated during the period of 7 (i.e. those constructed, completed or renovated between February 4th 1984 to Feb. 4th 2004) will instantly lose Chi strength. In feng shui terms, this means a severe curtailment of good fortune.

For this reason alone, it is worthwhile to seriously consider changing the Chi period of your home. This means changing your house, office or building into a period of 8 house, office or building.

This does **not** mean that you **must** change the Chi of your house, office or building into Period 8 Chi. What it does mean is that you must consider whether it will benefit and protect you to change. This requires you to analyse the flying star natal charts of your home based on **both** Period 7 and Period 8 charts.

38

When you analyse your house in terms of the two period charts, you will be able to see which period chart will bring you better luck based on the way the rooms in your house have already been laid out. And then you can determine whether or not it will benefit you to change your house into a period 8 house.

To make a sound decision, you will need to analyse how **both** the Period 7 and Period 8 charts affect the Chi distribution of your house. This is particularly important for those of you who live in houses or condominiums with swimming pools. Large pools of water exert important influences on your money luck, as well as your relationship luck. Remember that when water is placed incorrectly, it can cause you to lose money. Or when there is a pool where an auspicious mountain star occurs, **the mountain will fall into the water**, thereby destroying your relationship luck.

In the rest of this book, I will be presenting detailed analyses of all the Period 7 and Period 8 charts. This should make it very easy for you to eventually understand how to go about making the analyses of your own house yourself.

Examining the examples being given will also give you ideas on how you can improve the luck of your house using different solutions. Indeed, if you read this book in its entirety, you will know if it is better to stay on in your present home or if it would benefit you to find another house. Remember that in the end, it is your own judgment that should prevail.

Finally, those of you contemplating buying a new house or renovating your old house will find this book invaluable in helping you tap the auspicious wealth and relationship stars of the new period of 8.

What is a Flying Star Chart?

THIS IS A FLYING STAR CHART OF A PERIOD 7 HOUSE FACING SOUTH 1

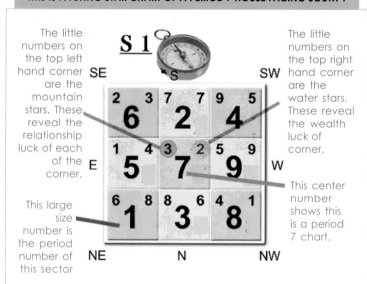

The little numbers on the top left hand corner are the mountain stars. These reveal the relationship luck of each of the corner.

The little numbers on the top right hand corner are the water stars. These reveal the wealth luck of corner.

This large size number is the period number of this sector

This center number shows this is a period 7 chart.

Here is what a flying star chart looks like. It has nine grids to represent the **nine palaces** of any home. These are the eight direction sectors on the sides plus the center. There are three numbers in each of the nine palaces. The large center number of each palace

is the **period star number** of that sector. The small number on the right in each palace is the **water star number**, which governs financial and wealth luck. The small number on the left in each palace is the **mountain star number**, which governs relationship luck. Please study the chart above and try to familiarise yourself with it.

F lying star charts reveal a great deal of information and this school of feng shui has often been likened to predictive Chinese numerology. This is because each of the numbers can signify many things about the luck of the sector and how this affects the residents residing in that sector.

Thus when bad star numbers **fly into bedrooms**, those residing there are sure to feel its effects. When bad star numbers occupy the facing palace where the main door is located, everyone in the house experiences bad luck. Likewise, when good star numbers are found here, everyone in the house benefits.

Remember that in Flying Star feng shui, we are talking about the feng shui of the whole house. It is **very different** from the practice of the KUA directions under Eight Mansions feng shui, which is a personalized method of feng shui. Thus the ideal would be to have excellent flying star numbers in your bedroom (irrespective of whether the bedroom location harmonizes with your KUA directions); and then to be able to position your bed such that you tap your **sheng chi** or other good KUA direction as you sleep. Please do not mix up personalised feng shui using individual directions with Flying Star feng shui, which applies to the whole house.

The Numbers in a Flying Star Chart

The numbers of a flying star chart indicate all the nuances of luck that apply to every sector, and depending on whether it is the period, water or mountain star, the numbers suggest indications of wealth luck, relationship luck or overall luck – or all three. Single numbers can be enhanced and magnified, or exhausted and killed by the other numbers that occupy the grid along with it.

Y ou will see that each of the palaces of the chart refers to a compass location in the house or building. The chart usually applies to the whole building and because of this, those of you living in apartments or condominiums will need to use the attributes of the **whole building** to determine the correct natal chart.

The star numbers in every sector, singly and in combination, offer important clues to the luck of the sector. Thus the numbers of the chart reveal the main problems encountered

by residents. Afflictions such as illnesses, difficulties in the marriage, quarrels and misunderstandings, as well as loss of money and wealth luck, all show up in the chart, especially when the correct chart has been identified for the house. This is what makes Flying Star feng shui so astoundingly accurate.

When you use the correct chart to analyse your home, it will reveal all your problems with money, health, relationships, children or whatever it is that is troubling you. It can explain

quarrels between spouses, it can show why your daughters cannot get married, why you cannot conceive a child, why you are losing money and so forth.

It can likewise reveal why your business is doing so well, or why your networking luck is so good, or why so many people are helping you.

The list of what a flying star chart can reveal about your luck and what it can foretell in terms of your health, wealth and relationship luck is so long and so accurate that this method of feng shui has often been labeled **predictive feng shui**.

In addition, the flying star chart can also be expanded to include the annual as well as monthly numbers, thereby giving pretty accurate indications of any severe forthcoming afflictions. Tracking the monthly and annual star numbers of your house chart will thus enable you to be forewarned.

For instance, when you know the illness star number 2 is flying into your bedroom next month, you can take action to control that affliction and thus avoid getting sick. Or when the loss-causing number 5 star flies into the sector where your main door is located, you can similarly take action to disarm the affliction.

In the same way that we practise annual and monthly feng shui updates, it is possible to also update our feng shui to take into the account the changes that period 8 will bring.

This book will focus on this important aspect of Flying Star, to help you generate the options that you and everyone else will face from the year 2004 and beyond. Then you can decide whether or not it is worth your while to change your house period. If you decide to transform your house into a period 8 house, later chapters of this book will show you how to do it.

How to Analyse a Flying Star Chart

There are six easy steps to the correct analysis of a flying star chart. Start by making sure you are using the correct chart for your house. Next, learn the best way to superimpose the chart onto the layout of your house. Step three requires the single numbers to be analysed. Step four looks at the combinations of numbers to see it there are any "specials". Step five looks at the combination of the water and mountain star numbers with the period numbers. Each of the three stars also has different strengths and holds other special meanings. Finally, step six involves Five Element analysis.

step 1 Determine which of the period 7 charts applies to your house. I am assuming that everyone reading this book is staying in a Period 7 house (i.e. that your house was built or renovated between February 4th 1984 to February 4th 2004). Determine the correct chart by correctly identifying the **facing direction of your house**. This can be a little tricky, but with some practice, you should soon be able to do this with accuracy.

step 2 Determine the most meaningful way to superimpose the sector numbers onto the house layout plan. This part of the exercise requires experience. There are different ways to demarcate the flying star sectors in a house, but again, after you go through all the examples in this book, you should get a pretty good feel for this part of the practice.

step 3 Next, identify the period, mountain and water stars and get a general "feel" for where their respective good numbers are located and where the affliction numbers are located. This will give you a general idea of the "luck" of the house. Remember that good water star numbers indicate good wealth luck and good mountain star numbers indicate good relationship luck.

step 4 Look out for the "specials" in the chart that indicate exceptional good luck. These specials include numbers that combine as a "**sum-of-ten**" or three numbers occurring in combinations that represent the "**Period or Parent String**" or as the "**Pearl String**". These specials will be indicated in the coming examples, which you should read as tutorials. You will discover that many of the charts seem to look quite similar in that many combinations occur frequently. The key to successful

analysis is of course to be able to read and analyse the numbers, as well as to correctly superimpose the numbers onto the different rooms of the house.

step 5 Study the combination of the water and mountain star numbers in each grid and see which star dominates in terms of their elements. This gives you an idea of whether money or relationships will dominate the luck of the residents who reside in that sector. Also study the combination of water with period, and mountain with period stars.

step 6 Finally, do investigate the five element (wu xing) analysis to determine the effects of the numbers in each of the sectors. Every number and sector has an equivalent element. Note that productive relationships between the numbers and sectors are always to be preferred to destructive relationships.

Determining the Correct Chart

This is a very important step to get right. If you use the wrong chart to analyse the Chi distribution of your house, the results will not be correct. Worse, you will be placing all your symbols in the incorrect corners rendering them ineffective at best, and harmful at worse.

Since we are at the tail end of the period of 7, it is quite safe to assume that most of us live in period 7 houses. This means the house was either built or was last renovated between February 4th 1984 and February 4th 2004, i.e. in the last twenty years. So getting the period right is not so difficult.

What is more challenging is to make sure that you get the **facing direction** of the house correct. This is because the flying star chart of any house is based on its facing direction. This usually means the facing direction of the main door, although it is not always the case that the door direction is the house facing direction. In many modern homes and buildings, the facing direction of the main door may not necessarily be the facing direction of the house (e.g. in modular and irregular shaped homes).

What makes the facing direction a controversial issue is that feng shui experts do not have a consensus view on the matter. Most are in agreement that one should look at a house carefully before deciding, so here are some suggestions for you to take note of to help you determine the facing direction of your house.

1. The facing direction is said to be facing the source of greatest **yang** energy, which can be a road, a market or even a city view.

2. Some experts believe that the facing direction is where the house faces the best unencumbered and most spectacular view. This can mean your balcony or living room patio facing a valley.

3. Others maintain that the facing direction is where the house is facing a "bright hall" or open ground.

The above descriptions do suggest that the facing direction of any house or building depends on its elevation and structure. For many houses, of course, the facing direction is usually obvious to an experienced eye. But modular-style houses or mansions that are surrounded by a 360-degree panoramic view can pose quite a challenge even to the most expert practitioner.

Personally, I have discovered that whenever I am in doubt, I will analyse the house according to several charts and match these with the experience and history of the residents in the house. This usually gives a good indication of which chart is the one that applies to the house. This is because the flying star chart is especially good at pinpointing the sectors that are afflicted with sickness, quarrelsome or burglary stars.

In fact, I find this to be such an excellent way of pinpointing the correct chart that I usually use a couple of charts to analyse the history of residents before I will say for sure which chart is the correct one. It is more work, of course, but doing it this way has greatly improved the accuracy and potency of my practice of Flying Star feng shui.

Superimposing the Chart

Once again there is no consensus amongst practising feng shui experts regarding the best way to superimpose the flying star chart onto the layout plan of houses. The single greatest difference is that some experts use the **pie chart** method which divides the sectors of a house according to a circular compass, while others use the nine sector grid method that resemble the Lo Shu square of numbers.

Personally, I prefer to use the nine-sector grid method to demarcate the sectors of any house. This method holds more logic for me, since the Lo Shu square plays such a big part in the theory of Flying Star feng shui. In addition, I find it simply makes more sense to divide the Chi energy of a house in this manner, as it is more practical, seeing that most houses have rectangular or square rooms rather than shaped as piece of pie-slice rooms.

But the controversy surrounding the question of superimposing

the numbers onto the house does not end there. Practising experts differ in their view of how the sectors themselves are demarcated. I have watched veteran practitioners divide house and room floor plans into nine equal grids and assign the corresponding numbers onto each of the grids, ignoring the real walls that separate the rooms of the house. This method can prove quite challenging if more than one set of sector numbers "rule" the luck of that room.

Thus I prefer to adopt the second approach, which is to

look at the natural barriers already existing in a home. I thus separate the sectors using the compass, but I am also mindful of the physical walls that divide up the sectors of the house.

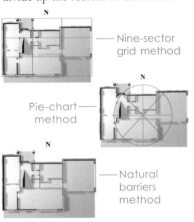

Nine-sector grid method

Pie-chart method

Natural barriers method

Over the years, I have discovered that this method offers the most accurate reading of the luck of any home. It is also the method that allows me maximum leeway with my use of numbers in maximising my luck. I can then create **wide, open spaces** in my home to tap the good numbers and little **prison rooms** to lock up the bad numbers! This is how I have maximised the good fortune Chi in my own home, and I discovered it works beautifully!

FOR APARTMENTS

Those living in apartments must use the **facing entrance of the whole building** to determine the correct chart for your apartment. Then you superimpose the chart onto your apartment according to the compass locations. Do not use the facing direction of your apartment door to determine the chart. However, IF you have a large picture window with a view and thus a major source of yang energy, AND you live on the 9th floor and above, then the facing direction of your balcony or patio with the unencumbered view will be the direction you take to determine your flying star chart.

The Meanings of the Numbers

There are many classical texts on the subject of numbers in feng shui and it is impossible to take note of every little nuance of every single number or combination of numbers. I believe it is sufficient to take note of the most important meanings of each of the nine numbers. Thus the dangerous numbers are 5 and 2 and in the period of 8, the number 7 is also dangerous. The number 3 is quarrelsome. The good numbers are 1, 6 and 8, with 8 being the luckiest. Here is a quick run down of what each number indicates.

The lucky numbers 1, 6 and 8
The three luckiest numbers are 1, 6 and 8. These are described as the white numbers. Of the three numbers, **8** is the luckiest, and wherever it shows up, it activates the Chi of the star it is. Using this guideline, many feng shui masters have identified the **water star 8** as being especially powerful in generating wealth luck when it is activated. The other numbers 1 and 6 are also lucky numbers. The number 1

means the first in the series. 1 also stands for career and income - generating potential. The number 6 signifies luck from heaven.

The number 9
This is a magnifying number. It multiplies good luck as well as bad luck. On its own, it is a lucky star, but its energy has not yet ripened. When it does, after 2024, the number 9 will become amazingly powerful. In the Period 7 and 8 charts, the

number 9 is to be particularly feared when it strengthens the bad stars 2 and 5.

The number 2

This is the illness star of the Flying Star system. It makes residents more vulnerable to common cold, cough, flu and other viruses. However, when it is strengthened by 9, or when it occurs in an earth element sector (such as the NE or SW of your house), it becomes extremely dangerous. When it is combined with the 5, the negative Chi generated by the combination becomes unbearably unpleasant.

The number 5

In Flying Star feng shui, the number 5 is known as the **wu wang** or the five yellow. It is considered the most dangerous of the nine numbers and when the annual 5 flies into any sector, it brings loss and sickness. In any house chart, the appearance of 5 can be contained by hanging

six-rod all-metal windchimes in the afflicted sector.

The number 4

This is a good star number. It is also the romantic and literary star, bringing extreme good fortune for writers and scholars. Its benefits are enhanced when combined with the number 1, although this combination can sometimes lead to sexual scandals caused by illicit love affairs.

The number 7

This was lucky in the past twenty years, but turns unlucky in 2004 when its true nature reverts. In the new period, the number 7 brings loss, burglary and violence.

The number 3

This is the star number which signifies hostility, quarrels, misunderstandings and lawsuits. At its worse, it brings problems with authorities and fierce fighting amongst friends and colleagues. Overcome with fire energy.

The Auspicious Specials

In addition to the meanings of the numbers, you should also be on the lookout for the **auspicious specials**. These are unique combinations of numbers that create the potential for residents of any house having such **specials** to enjoy the most amazingly good feng shui.

These combinations occur rarely – only one or two charts in each period have them. In some periods they do not occur at all. I shall be alerting you to the charts where these combinations occur. If you are building a new house and are able to build a house with this kind of chart, you should definitely strive to do so, irrespective of whether the direction corresponds to your personal KUA direction or not.

These specials include two numbers that combine into a "**sum-of-ten**" in every sector, or three numbers occurring in combinations that represent the "**Period or Parent String**" or the "**Pearl String**", again in every sector. Either of these two sets of specials would be considered outstanding feng shui when properly used and activated. Finally, there are the four **Ho Tu** combination numbers that also bring exceptional good fortune.

These **auspicious specials** are said to override any bad numbers that may appear in any sector, and have the power to bring exceptional good fortune, abundance and wealth.

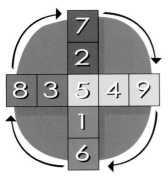

The four Ho Tu combinations of numbers that bring good luck

Residents will enjoy excellent descendants luck and amazingly good relationship and mentor luck.

You will find that in period 8, there are two facing direction houses that contain the auspicious specials and for this reason alone, those of you fortunate enough to have houses that fit these charts should definitely change the period of your house to that of period 8. If you can successfully change the period of your house, you would then be able to tap just about the best charts in the period 8.

These charts occur for houses that have a facing direction of **Northeast** or **Southwest**. For this reason, it can categorically be stated that all houses facing or sitting on the SW/NE axis will enjoy excellent good fortune. It does not matter which of the three sub-sectors of these directions your house faces. As long as it faces or sits along this axis direction, and you tap the distribution of Chi correctly, period 8 will bring you loads of great good fortune.

Once again it is necessary to stress that this diagnosis is based on Flying Star feng shui, and **ignores Eight Mansions**. So even if you belong to the East group of auspicious directions, having this West group axis of NE/SW in your house will still bring you and your family some truly wonderful good luck.

The Water and Mountain Stars

When you read a flying star chart with the idea of activating the two most important types of luck - **wealth** and **relationship** luck - the way to do it is to see which of the water and mountain stars in your house chart have the auspicious number 8. It is the sectors that have the water star 8 and the mountain star 8 where the best wealth and relationship luck potential exists.

Then you will know where to build your water and mountain feature. When you do this correctly and the Chi created by your water and mountain feature is able to enter your home, you will then enjoy truly excellent feng shui.

Activating the auspicious water and mountains star sectors is one of the most powerful ways to activate good feng shui. When you study the period 7 and period 8 charts, you will find that as soon as the period changes, the placement of the auspicious water and mountain stars **do not change** for your house **unless you change the period of your house**. This is really important for you to understand.

As long as you do not change the period of your house, then the original period 7 chart will continue to define the feng shui Chi distribution of your home.

54

So the water and mountain star numbers also do not change. Only the meanings of some of the numbers will change (e.g. the number 7 which brought so much good luck in period 7 will now bring bloodshed, robbery and violence. And the number 3, which brings hostility energy in period 7 becomes lucky in period 8 because 3 has a special relationship with the number 8.)

This also means that if you have already built a pool where your water star 8 is located and a mountain feature such as a stone wall where your mountain star 8 is located, and you had made millions all through period 7, it does not mean you will suddenly suffer loss in 2004 when the period changes.

But it *does* mean that the energy of your chart has lost vitality. You will discover that the good times and good luck will start to dry up. You should really study the period 8 chart that applies to your house and see how it will affect what you have already built in your home.

If you wish, you can delay changing your house to a period 8 house for a few years to see how your luck is affected in period 8. If the wealth luck of your family suffers, then you must certainly consider changing your house to a period 8 house.

The same thing if your health or relationship luck suffers a loss of strength. Remember that irrespective of how the charts compare, all period 7 houses will lose energy when the period changes.

This is something that cannot be ignored. Thus everyone who makes the decision not to change the period of their house must take steps to reactivate the Chi energy of their homes.

Analysing the Elements of the Chart

In Flying Star feng shui, five-element analysis of the chart reveals nuances about the luck of house sectors. The rule here is always asking yourself what **element** is flying into the sector. Each sector also has an element. When the incoming element **produces** the sector element, the effect is good; but when the incoming element destroys or exhausts the sector element, the effect is a weakening of energy of the sector's element, and this is not good.

The easy part about formula feng shui is that the analysis of meanings and cures under all the different methods are based on the attributes of the eight sides of the Later Heaven Pa Kua. Once you learn up the numbers, elements and directions of each of the eight sides of the Pa Kua, you will be able to practise many different methods of feng shui enhancement.

Look at the illustration shown on the facing page. Note that each side of the Pa Kua, also referred to as a KUA, corresponds to one of the eight directions.

Next, look at the number assigned to each side. Finally, memorise the element that has been assigned to each side. From this table, you will be able to undertake element analysis of the numbers flying into the different sectors under Flying Star.

PRODUCTIVE CYCLE

Wood produces fire, fire produces earth, earth produces metal, metal produces water and water produces wood.

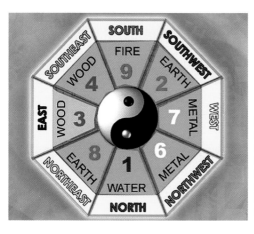

Study the numbers, colours and elements associated with each side of the PA KUA as shown here.

DESTRUCTIVE CYCLE

Wood destroys earth, earth destroys water, water destroys fire, fire destroys metal and metal destroys wood.

Once you know the cycles, you can undertake element analysis with no problem. Thus, when the number 1 which is water flies into the Southeast, the incoming number will enhance the Southeast. This is because water produces wood. If it flies into the South, it destroys the energy of the South. This is because water destroys fire. Likewise when the metal star number 6 flies into the East, it destroys the wood energy of the East - and so on. So study the illustration above and commit the directions, numbers and elements to memory. This is the correlation between the three attributes under the Later Heaven Arrangement of the Pa Kua.

57

Analysing The Period 7 Charts

Chapter 2

Analysing the Period 7 Charts

TUI

THE LAKE

In this chapter, we take a close look at the Period 7 charts. The important indications for each house chart are highlighted to examine what kind of Chi energy affects each sector according to the numbers in the sector. You can study detailed Period 7 analysis of house plans in Chapter 5 of my book *Feng Shui for Interiors*. For those keen on mastering Flying Star feng shui, I recommend that you read that book in conjunction with this book to give you an easier understanding of flying star charts.

Please note that any feng shui analysis is always more complete when a proper onsite investigation is done. Truly, it is impossible to take account of the many things that can and does impinge on the energy of a house. So a full onsite investigation is always recommended, as it always gives us more information to work with. Then the forms, shapes, landscapes, design features, flow of energies and so forth can be studied in conjunction with the Flying Star numbers. The summaries

of how the numbers of a flying star chart affect the space they occupy will give any amateur feng shui practitioner an excellent template to work with. It is a good starting point to improving the feng shui of any house.

Examine the sixteen charts given here in this chapter. You can look at all the charts or go straight to the chart that applies to your home.

Study how the numbers interact with each other. Also look

60

at how the numbers are superimposed onto house plans. It is a good idea to study a couple of charts that may correspond to the probable facing direction of your house and see if the information revealed by the charts correspond with your own experiences. If it does, then you are looking at an accurate map of your house Chi distribution. This is the essence of advanced feng shui, the kind used by bona fide feng shui masters.

I discovered this is an excellent way to see which chart really applies to any house. Much like the wonderful astrologer who looked at my life chart many years ago, and was so incredibly accurate in charting the twists and turns of my life that were to take place. Before he started, he made some calculations and then asked me three questions before proceeding. He wanted to know if I had two brothers, if my parents were still alive (then) and if I had three moles on my hands and feet. It was

only after I had replied in the affirmative to all three questions that he was satisfied he had worked out a correct life chart for me. Then only did he begin his reading.

> You can use this same method to see if the chart you select as applying to your house is the correct one.

Next, if your house is facing the first sub-direction, also study the chart that faces the second sub-direction, since the difference can usually be only a few degrees. This will also give you a good idea if the first sub-direction or the second/third sub-directions apply to your house (e.g. is your house facing South 1, or South 2/3?) And also - which sub-direction would work better for the layout of your house! Note that sometimes, with only a little effort, you can change the sub-direction of your house facing direction to change the entire Chi distribution of your home.

Check your Facing Direction

To select the correct flying star chart that applies to your house, it is necessary to determine the facing direction of your house (or apartment) correctly. This means the facing direction selected must be the correct one. This requires you to take your compass readings correctly.

Note that in Flying Star feng shui, we divide the 360 degrees of the compass into 24 directions of fifteen degrees each. The charts are based on which of these 24 directions your house faces. We call these the first, second and third sub-directions of the 8 main directions of the compass.

For easy reference, the names & degrees of the subdirections of the 8 directions are summarised in the chart here. Also indicated are the **emptiness lines**.

These are the **special** directions you must always **avoid** facing. They are taboo lines! If your house is facing an emptiness line, place 2 metal rulers near the door to modify the direction slightly.

THE DEGREES OF THE 24 MOUNTAINS

NOTE EMPTINESS LINES

SOUTHEAST	SOUTH	SOUTHWEST
112.5 - 157.5	157.5 - 202.5	202.5 - 247.5
SE 1: 112.5 TO 127.5	S1: 157.5 TO 172.5	SW 1: 202.5 TO 217.5
SE 2/3: 127.5 TO 157.5	S2/3: 172.5 TO 202.5	SW2/3: 217.5 TO 247.5
EMPTINESS 157.5	EMPTINESS 202.5	EMPTINESS 247.5
shen shun tze	ping wu ting	wei kun sen

EAST		WEST
67.5 - 112.5	names of 24 mountains move clockwise	247.5 - 292.5
E1: 67.5 TO 82.5		W1: 247.5 TO 262.5
E2/3: 82.5 TO 112.5		W2/3: 262.5 TO 292.5
EMPTINESS 112.5		EMPTINESS 292.5

(left margin, rotated:) sma mau yi

(right margin, rotated:) ken yu sin

NORTHEAST	NORTH	NORTHWEST
22.5 - 67.5	337.5 - 22.5	292.5 - 337.5
NE1: 22.5 - 37.5	N1: 337.7 TO 352.5	NW1: 292.5 TO 307.5
NE2/3: 37.5 TO 67.5	N2/3: 352.5 TO 22.5	NW2/3: 307.5 TO 337.5
EMPTINESS 67.5	EMPTINESS 22.5	EMPTINESS 337.5
yiu gen choh	kway cher zen	hai chien shih

PERIOD 7 facing SOUTH 1

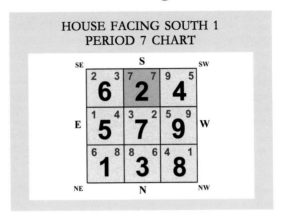

HOUSE FACING SOUTH 1
PERIOD 7 CHART

Note that it is almost always auspicious to live in a South-facing house. In Period 7, it enjoys the double 7. This house would benefit from a water feature placed in the Northeast sector of the property. Inside the home, placing a bubbling water bowl (with or without fish) in the NE of the living room will be good. The West and SW sectors are afflicted by the 5/9 combination and these need to be overcome with metal wind chimes. The house benefits enormously with the mountain star 8 at the back. Building a brick or stonewall at the back of the house would have been very beneficial.

This house must consider changing to Period 8.

ANALYSIS OF NUMBERS

FRONT OF HOUSE

SOUTHEAST	SOUTH	SOUTHWEST
2 6 3	facing palace	**9 4 5**
	7 2 7	
Hostile wood 3 as the water star. Must be suppressed with yin fire. Reduce illness earth 2 with metal energy.	Auspicious double 7 in the facing palace brings good fortune in period 7. Must change to period 8	Unlucky earth 5 brings loss of wealth. It is strengthened by fire 9. Control the 5 with yang metal. Hang windchimes.
EAST	CENTER	WEST
1 5 4	**+ 3 7 2 -**	**5 9 9**
Water star 4 is enhanced as it is helped by 1 posing as a mountain star. This sector enjoys wealth, health and children luck.	Two unlucky stars locked in the center Place metal energy to control illness earth 2 and hostile wood 3.	Mountain star 5 is unlucky for family. It is strengthened by the fire 9. Must control 5 with yang metal.
NORTHEAST	NORTH	NORTHWEST
6 1 8	sitting palace	**4 8 1**
	8 3 6	
Auspicious water star 8 is exhausted by metal 6. Activate with water. Use crystals to strengthen earth Chi here.	Auspicious mountain star 8 supports the house. Activate with virtual mountain. Place crystal cluster or wall behind.	Lucky water star 1 is exhausted by wood 4. Money luck gets blocked. Use metal to control wood and enhance water. Activate water.

PERIOD 7 facing SOUTH 2 or 3

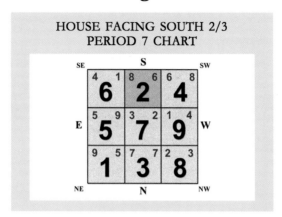

This is a **sum-of-ten** house, which means it is a very auspicious house indeed as this situation does not occur often. This is one of the very **auspicious special** combinations of numbers. Here, the period stars combine with the mountain stars in every sector to add up to a **sum-of-ten**, bringing excellent health, relationship, family, children and mentor luck to residents. The house also benefited from the double 7 stars at the back of the house, giving solid support to the residents. The auspicious water star 8 has flown to the Southwest in front, while the mountain star 8 has flown to the South in front.

This house must consider changing to Period 8 because of the double 7.

SUM-OF-TEN WITH MOUNTAIN STAR

FRONT OF HOUSE

SOUTHEAST 461	SOUTH facing palace 826	SOUTHWEST 648
Lucky water star 1 is exhausted by wood 4. Money luck gets blocked. Use metal to control wood and enhance water. Activate water.	Auspicious mountain star 8 in the facing palace. Activate mountain with boulders & crystals for extreme good fortune.	Auspicious water star 8 is exhausted by metal 6. Activate with water. Use crystals to strengthen earth Chi here.
EAST 559	CENTER - 372 +	WEST 194
Mountain star 5 is unlucky for family. It is strengthened by the fire 9. Must control 5 with yang metal.	Sum-of-ten chart enhancing mountain star brings great good fortune for family, health children & love. Activate with mountain.	Activate sum-of-ten and auspicious 1 as the mountain star. This brings extreme good fortune for daughters of family.
NORTHEAST 915	NORTH sitting palace 737	NORTHWEST 382
Unlucky earth 5 brings loss of wealth. It is strengthened by fire 9. Control the 5 with yang metal. Hang windchimes.	Auspicious double 7 in the sitting palace. Activate sum-of-ten by enhancing mountain star with mountain.	Hostle wood 3 as the water star must be suppressed with yin fire. Reduce illness earth 2 with metal energy.

PERIOD 7 facing NORTH 1

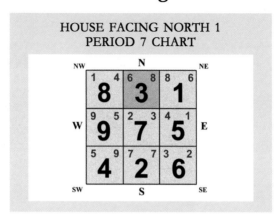

This chart above has been "turned" to bring the North palace to the top for easy reference. It appears different from the chart on the right, but it is the same chart. I do this to get you used to **turning** the charts to accommodate the way your house plan may have been drawn. It is always easier to analyse a chart when you redraw it such that the chart is viewed from the same orientation as the house plan. In this chart note that all the auspicious numbers are at the front of the house. And there is a double 7 at the back. If this is your house, decide if this or N2/3 is better suited to your house layout of rooms.

This house must consider changing to period 8.

ANALYSIS OF NUMBERS

SOUTHEAST	SOUTH	SOUTHWEST
3 6 2	sitting palace **7 2 7**	**5 4 9**
Illness earth 2 as water star hurts family finances. Good thing wood 3 controls the 2 even though 3 brings misfortunes. Suppress with yin gold.	Auspicious double 7 to support the house. Activate mountain star with virtual mountain & crystal cluster.	The fire 9 as the water star strengthens unlucky earth 5, magnifying misfortunes in family relationships. Reduce with yang metal windchimes.
EAST	CENTER	WEST
4 5 1	**- 2 7 3 +**	**9 9 5**
Lucky water star 1 must be activated by water. Wood 4 brings family luck, but too much water can lead to scandals.	Two unlucky stars locked in the center. Toilet in the center is OK in this house. No water or mountain image to be placed here.	Unlucky earth 5 causes loss of wealth, failure and business problems. It is strengthened by the fire 9. Use metal to control.
NORTHEAST	NORTH	NORTHWEST
8 1 6	facing palace **6 3 8**	**1 8 4**
Auspicious mountain star 8 should be activated by mountain. Dragon image. Water star 6 is metal, enhanced by the 8.	Very auspicious water star 8 at facing palace. Activate with water. Suppress metal 6 with fire energy.	Wood 4 as the water star brings prosperity & success. Strengtheend by auspicious water 1 as the mountain star. Activate the mountain star.

FRONT OF HOUSE

PERIOD 7 facing NORTH 2 or 3

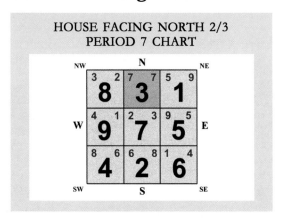

The chart above has also been "turned" to bring the North palace to the top. Please get used to turning the chart to facilitate your analysis.

You can see from this chart that the Double 7 has flown to the front of the house, and flanking the facing palace are troublesome star numbers 3/2 in the NW and 5/9 in the NE. The house also has the quarelsome 3 and illness 2 in the center. All the auspicious rooms are at the back of the house so there is a possibility of them being wasted as maids rooms. You might want to consider changing to a North 1 facing direction.

Should definitely consider changing to a period 8 house.

ANALYSIS OF NUMBERS

SOUTHEAST 1 6 4	SOUTH sitting palace 6 2 8	SOUTHWEST 8 4 6
Wood 4 as the water star brings prosperity. Strengthened by lucky water 1 as the mountain star. Activate the mountain star.	Very auspicious water star 8 to support house. Activate with water. Suppress metal 6 with fire energy.	Auspicious mountain star 8 should be activated by mountain or dragon image. Water star 6 is metal enhanced by the 8. Can activate water here.
EAST 9 5 5	CENTER + 2 7 3 -	WEST 4 9 1
Unlucky earth 5 causes loss of wealth, failure & business problems. It is strengthened by the fire 9. Use metal to control and reduce the effect.	Two unlucky stars locked in the center. Toilet in the center is OK in this house. No water or mountain image to be placed here.	Lucky water star 1 and wood 4 brings family luck. Since too much water can lead to scandals, better to activate mountain star.
NORTHEAST 5 1 9	NORTH facing palace 7 3 7	NORTHWEST 3 8 2
Fire 9 as the water star strengthens the unlucky earth 5, magnifying misfortunes in family relationships. Control with metal windchime. Avoid living here.	Auspicious double 7 in the facing palace. Activate water star with real water. Must change to period 8.	Illness earth 2 as water star hurts family finances. Good that wood 3 controls the 2 even though 3 brings misfortunes. Suppress with yin gold.

FRONT OF HOUSE

PERIOD 7 facing EAST 1

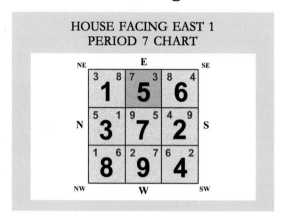

HOUSE FACING EAST 1
PERIOD 7 CHART

This smaller chart above has been "turned" to bring the East palace to the top. If your plan is drawn with the entrance at the bottom use the chart on the right to analyse. East-facing houses are afflicted by the period 5 star which always brings some kind of affliction. As a result, the water star 5 flies to the center of the house and is enhanced by the magnifying energy of 9.

The advantage of East 1 facing houses is that the two front sectors of NE and SE have the auspicious water and mountain star 8 respectively. If you had cleverly activated these two sectors with a large pool in the NE and a mountain feature in the SE, you might want to consider retaining this as a period 7 house.

If you had not, you should consider changing it to period 8.

ANALYSIS OF NUMBERS

SOUTHWEST	WEST	NORTHWEST
6 4 2	sitting palace 2 9 7	1 8 6
Unlucky earth 2 as the water star brings illness. Fortunately, metal 6 exhausts the 2. Activate mountain star with crystal cluster.	Auspicious water star 7 is blocked by earth 2. Use metal to overcome the 2 and place a water feature to activate.	Lucky water 1 brings family luck as the mountain star. Metal 6 enhances it. Activate with mountain image.
SOUTH	CENTER	NORTH
4 2 9	+ 9 7 5 +	5 3 1
Fire 9 as water star brings luck, strengthened by wood 4. But it brings distant prosperity. Activate mountain star with mountain.	Unlucky earth 5 as the water star is strengthened by fire 9. Lock up the stars or use metal windchimes to control the 5.	Lucky water 1 brings money luck but is blocked by unlucky earth 5, as the mountain star 5 brings illness & misfortune. Control with windchimes.
SOUTHEAST	EAST	NORTHEAST
8 6 4	facing palace 7 5 3	3 1 8
Wood star 4 brings money luck. But mountain star 8 is more auspicious. Activate with mountain for family & relationship luck.	Hostile wood 3 water star is controlled by metal 7, which reduces its effect. Activate mountain star with mountain.	Auspicious water star 8. Activate with water. Wood 3 exhausts the 8. Use earth or yin metal to control the wood 3 star.

FRONT OF HOUSE

PERIOD 7 facing EAST 2 or 3

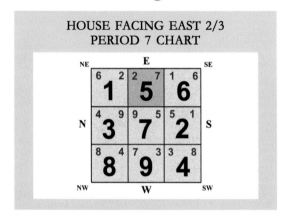

HOUSE FACING EAST 2/3
PERIOD 7 CHART

This smaller chart above has been "turned" to bring the East palace to the top. If your plan shows the entrance below, use the larger chart on the right to analyse.

This East 2/3 facing house does not enjoy the same lucky stars as the East 1 house in the front. In fact, the lucky water and mountain stars have flown to the back of the house where it could be "wasted" as the kitchen and maid rooms are usually placed here at the back. The facing palace of this chart also shows a deadly combination of numbers for period 8 i.e. 2/5/7... and this spells danger in period 8.

You must seriously consider changing this house to period 8.

ANALYSIS OF NUMBERS

SOUTHWEST 3 4 8	WEST sitting palace 7 9 3	NORTHWEST 8 8 4
Auspicious water star 8. Activate with water. Wood 3 exhausts the 8. Use earth or yin metal to control the wood 3 star.	Hostile wood 3 water star is contolled by metal 7, which reduces its effect. Activate mountain star with mountain.	Wood star 4 brings money luck. But mountain star 8 is more auspicious. Activate with mountain for family, relationship & health luck.
SOUTH 5 2 1	CENTER + 9 7 5 +	NORTH 4 3 9
Lucky water 1 brings money luck, but is blocked by unlucky earth 5. As the mountain star, 5 brings illness & misfortune. Control with windchimes.	Unlucky earth 5 as the water star is strengthened by fire 9. Lock up the stars or use metal windchimes to control the 5.	Fire 9 as water star brings luck, strengthened by wood 4. But it brings distant prosperity. Activate mountain star with mountain.
SOUTHEAST 1 6 6	EAST facing palace 2 5 7	NORTHEAST 6 1 2
Lucky water 1 brings family luck as the mountain star. metal 6 enhances it. Activate with mountain image or crystal cluster.	Auspicious water star 7 is blocked by earth 2. Use metal to overcome the 2 & place a water feature to activate.	Unlucky earth 2 as the water star brings illness. Fortunately, metal 6 exhausts the 2. Strengthen metal energy here.

FRONT OF HOUSE

PERIOD 7 facing WEST 1

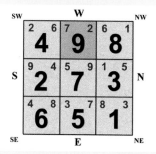

HOUSE FACING WEST 1
PERIOD 7 CHART

This smaller chart above has been "turned" to bring the West palace to the top. If your house plan is drawn with the entrance at the bottom, use the chart on the right to analyse. The numbers will then correspond to the orientation of West in your plan. This is for ease of analysis.

West 1 facing houses suffer from the affliction of the 5/9 in the center. The water star 8 is at the back (SE). Since this is also a good sector for water, place water here to activate wealth luck. The mountain star 8 is in the Northeast, also at the back of the house. A brick wall in this sector would be excellent feng shui. Compare this chart with the period 8 chart facing West 1 to decide which suits the layout of your house better.

ANALYSIS OF NUMBERS

NORTHEAST	EAST	SOUTHEAST
81**3**	sitting palace **3**5**7**	**4**6**8**
Auspicious mountain star 8. Activate with mountain image for family & relationship luck. Suppress wood 3 with yin fire energy.	Lucky water star 7 at the back. Activate with yin water which also diffuses hostile 3.	Auspicious water star 8 is exhausted by wood 4 as the mountain star. Activate with water. Water will bring money & relationship luck.
NORTH	CENTER	SOUTH
13**5**	- **5**7**9** -	**9**2**4**
Lucky mountain star 1 brings career luck. But earth 5 can cause loss of wealth. Control with metal windchimes or 7 coins.	Two dangerous numbers in the center of the home must be locked or controlled with 6 rod metal windchimes.	Water star is wood 4. This is exhausted by fire 9. Activate with real water. Mountain star 9 is also lucky. Activate with mountain.
NORTHWEST	WEST	SOUTHWEST
68**1**	facing palace **7**2**9**	**2**4**6**
Excellent water star 1 brings wealth luck & metal 6 strengthens this luck. Activate with real water. Place metal coins nearby.	Lucky 7 mountain star strengthened by earth 2. It exhausts illness effect of 2 as the water star. Activate with metal.	Metal 6 as water star has little strength. It is overcome by the earth 2 as the mountain star. Suppress 2 with metal energy. Hang windchimes.

FRONT OF HOUSE

PERIOD 7 facing WEST 2 or 3

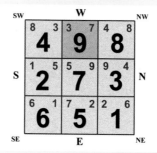

HOUSE FACING WEST 2/3
PERIOD 7 CHART

This smaller chart above has been "turned" to bring the West palace to the top. If your house plan is drawn with the entrance at the bottom, use the chart on the right. The numbers will then correspond to the orientation of west in your plan.

West 2/3 facing houses suffer from the affliction of the 5/9 in the center. The water star 8 is in front in the NW and the lucky mountain star 8 is in the SW, also at the front of the house. Having these two auspicious sectors at the front of the house flanking the West facing palace usually brings benefits to residents. To decide if you should change to a period 8 house, compare the luck implications on your house based on the features and room layouts you already have. Anyone thinking of extensive renovations, however, would benefit from changing to period 8.

ANALYSIS OF NUMBERS

NORTHEAST	EAST	SOUTHEAST
21**6**	sitting palace **7**5**2**	**66**1
Metal 6 as water star has little strength. It is overcome by the earth 2 as the mountain star. Suppress 2 with metal energy. Hang windchimes.	Lucky 7 mountain star strengthened by earth 2 in sitting palace is good. It exhausts illness effect of earth 2. Activate!	Excellent water star 1 brings wealth luck & metal 6 strengthens this luck. Activate with real water. Place metal coins nearby.
NORTH	CENTER	SOUTH
93**4**	- **5**7**9** -	**1**2**5**
Water star is wood 4. This is exhausted by fire 9. Activate with real water. Mountain star 9 is also lucky. Activate with mountain.	Two dangerous numbers in the center of the home must be locked up, or controlled with 6 rod metal windchimes.	Lucky mountain star 1 brings recognition luck. But earth 5 can cause loss of wealth. Control with metal windchimes or 7 coins.
NORTHWEST	WEST	SOUTHWEST
48**8**	facing palace **3**9**7**	**8**4**3**
Auspicious water star 8 is exhausted by wood 4 as the mountain star. Activate with water. Water will bring money & relationship luck.	Lucky water star 7 in the facing palace very lucky. Activate with yang water which causes 3 to "fall into water".	Auspicious mountain star 8. Activate with mountain image for family & relationship luck. Suppress wood 3 with yin fire energy.

FRONT OF HOUSE

PERIOD 7 facing SW 1

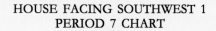

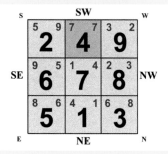

HOUSE FACING SOUTHWEST 1
PERIOD 7 CHART

This smaller chart above has been "turned" to bring the Southwest palace to the top. If your house plan is drawn with the entrance at the bottom, use the chart on your right for ease of analysis. Southwest facing charts enjoyed the double 7 either in the facing or in the sitting palace (depending on the subdirection) all through the period of 7. In a Southwest 1 house, it was in the front, bringing great good fortune to residents. The numbers of sectors to the left and right of the facing palace, however, have afflicted numbers. So, despite the good fortune, it was by no means a smooth ride. If you compare this chart with the period 8 chart for Southwest facing houses, you will see that the period 8 chart enjoys the **auspicious specials**.

All SW facing houses should definitely change to period 8!

PERIOD 7 - FACING SOUTHWEST 1

ANALYSIS OF NUMBERS

NORTH 6 3 8 Water star 8. Earth 8 is exhausted by 6 metal. Wealth luck is blocked. Strengthen 8 with fire, which overcomes metal.	**NORTHEAST** sitting palace 4 1 1 Water star 1. Water 1 is exhausted by wood 4. Wealth luck cannot materialise unless you place metal here.	**EAST** 8 5 6 Mountain star 8. Earth 8 is exhausted by metal 6. Relationship & health luck gets blocked. Place fire Chi here to enhance earth.
NORTHWEST 2 8 3 Illness star earth 2 pressed by wood 3. Use fire energy to control quarrelsome star 3. Use metal to control earth 2.	**CENTER** + 1 7 4 - Parent string numbers. Must not be enclosed. Wood 4 is enhanced by water 1. Success in writing materialises.	**SOUTHEAST** 9 6 5 Illness earth 5 is strengthened by fire 9. Use metal to exhaust 5. Use wood to support 9 to improve health, relationships & fertility.
WEST 3 9 2 Water star is earth 2, killed by quarrelsome wood 3. No wealth luck is possible. Use metal to control earth 2 to protect against loss of wealth.	**SOUTHWEST** facing palace 7 4 7 Double 7 at facing palace. Activate water star 7 with water. Activate mountain star 7 with mountain or crystals.	**SOUTH** 5 2 9 Water star is fire 9. It is exhausted by earth 5. Wealth luck gets blocked. Unlucky star 5 blocks relationship luck. Use metal to suppress 5.

FRONT OF HOUSE

PERIOD 7 facing SW 2 or 3

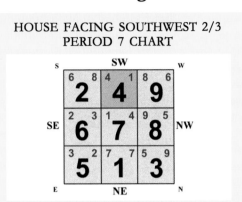

HOUSE FACING SOUTHWEST 2/3
PERIOD 7 CHART

This smaller chart above has been "turned" to bring the Southwest facing palace to the top. If your house plan is drawn with the entrance at the bottom, use the chart on the right with the numbers corresponding to the orientations of your plan. This is easier to analyse. Southwest 2/3 facing houses enjoy the auspicious # 8 water and mountain stars in the front of the house. The double 7 goes to the back of the house. Note that all Southwest facing houses have enormously lucky specials in terms of its combinations of numbers. Southwest houses sit Northeast, which is the corresponding direction of the period 8.

It is definitely recommended that SW facing houses should change to period 8.

PERIOD 7 - FACING SOUTHWEST 2 or 3

ANALYSIS OF NUMBERS

NORTH	NORTHEAST sitting palace	EAST
5**3**9	**7**1**7**	3**5**2
Water star is fire 9. It is exhausted by earth 5. Wealth luck gets blocked. Unlucky star 5 blocks relationship luck. Use metal to suppress the 5.	Double 7 in sitting palace. Activate water star 7 with water. Activate mountain star 7 with mountain or crystal cluster.	Water star is earth 2. Killed by quarrelsome wood 3. No wealth luck is possible. Use metal to control earth 2 to safeguard loss of wealth.
NORTHWEST	**CENTER**	**SOUTHEAST**
9**8**5	- 1**7**4 +	2**6**3
Illness earth 5 is strengthened by fire 9. Use metal to exhaust 5. Use wood to support 9 to improve health, relationships & fertility.	Parent string numbers. This area must not be enclosed. Wood 4 is enhanced by water 1. Success in writing materialises.	Illness star earth 2 pressed by wood 3. Use fire energy to control quarrelsome star 3. Use metal to control earth 2.
WEST	**SOUTHWEST** facing palace	**SOUTH**
8**9**6	4**4**1	6**2**8
Mountain star 8. Earth 8 is exhausted by metal 6. Relationship & health luck gets blocked. Place fire here to enhance earth.	Water star 1. Water 1 is exhausted by wood 4. Wealth luck cannot materialise unless metal is placed here.	Water star 8. Earth 8 is exhausted by 6 metal. Wealth luck is blocked. Strengthen 8 with fire, which overcomes metal.

FRONT OF HOUSE

PERIOD 7 facing NE 1

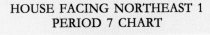

**HOUSE FACING NORTHEAST 1
PERIOD 7 CHART**

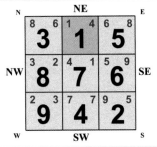

This smaller chart above has been "turned" to bring the Northeast palace to the top. If your house plan is drawn with the entrance at the bottom, use the chart on the right. The numbers then correspond to the orientation of Northeast in your plan. This is for ease of analysis. NE 1 facing houses have very similar charts to houses that face SW 2/3, in that the front part of the house enjoy excellent numbers including the auspicious water and mountain stars. Both sides of the house (SE and NW) have afflicted numbers which cause illness and disharmony. But these can be corrected.

All NE facing houses should definitely change to period of 8 to enjoy the benefit of superior Chi distribution in the house.

ANALYSIS OF NUMBERS

SOUTH 9**2**5 Unlucky earth 5 as water star enhanced by fire 9. Suppress with metal & water Use yin water & yang metal.	**SOUTHWEST** sitting palace 7**4**7 Double 7 excellent, but metal exhausts earth corner. Strengthen with fire. Activate with mountain.	**WEST** 2**9**3 Hostile wood 3 suppresses wealth luck. Illness star earth 2 is pressed by the earth 3. This is a metal sector, so both stars are under control.
SOUTHEAST 5**6**9 Strong fire 9 as water star but wealth luck blocked by earth 5. Use wood to control 5 & enhance 9. Wood aslo enhance this wood sector	**CENTER** - 4**7**1 + Parent string combination in center. Leave open. Wood 4 exhausts water 1. Wealth luck is exhausted. Strengthen with metal	**NORTHWEST** 3**8**2 Unlucky earth 2 is the water star. It is killed by wood 3. Mountain star 3 is exhausted in this metal sector. Place yin metal.
EAST 6**5**8 Lucky earth 8 brings wealth luck but blocked by metal 6. Use fire to enhance 8 and weaken 6. Improve health luck with earth energy.	**NORTHEAST** facing palace 1**1**4 Auspicious wood 4 is strengthened by water 1, bringing wealth luck. But health & relationships need metal to enhance.	**NORTH** 8**3**6 Lucky mountain star has earth 8. Marriage family health luck, but metal 6 exhausts 8. Strengthen with fire energy. Activate with a mountain symbol.

FRONT OF HOUSE

PERIOD 7 facing NE 2 or 3

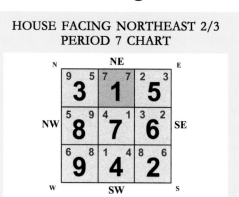

**HOUSE FACING NORTHEAST 2/3
PERIOD 7 CHART**

This smaller chart above has been "turned" to bring the Northeast palace to the top. If your house plan is drawn with the entrance at the bottom, use the chart on the right. The numbers then correspond to the orientation of Northeast in your plan. This is for ease of analysis. NE 2/3 facing houses enjoyed the double 7 in the facing palace which will turn unlucky and even dangerous in the period of 8. Note that the auspicious sectors with the auspicious water and mountain stars 8 are at the back of the house, where they are probably wasted with the location of the kitchen and maid rooms there.

It is definitely a good idea to change the house to a period of 8 house to take advantage of better numbers in the chart and to strengthen its Chi energy.

ANALYSIS OF NUMBERS

SOUTH 8 2 6 Lucky mountain star has earth 8. Marriage, family & health luck, but metal 6 exhausts 8. Strengthen with fire. Activate with mountain symbol.	**SOUTHWEST** sitting palace 1 4 4 Auspicious wood 4 is strengthened by water 1, bringing wealth luck. But health & relationship luck need metal to enhance.	**WEST** 6 9 8 Lucky earth 8 brings wealth luck, but this is blocked by the metal 6. Use fire to enhance 8 & weaken 6. Enhance for health with earth energy.
SOUTHEAST 3 6 2 Unlucky earth 2 is the water star. It is killed by wood 3. Control mountain star 3 with fire energy to exhaust & reduce anger.	**CENTER** + 4 7 1 - Parent string combination in center. Leave open. Wood 4 exhausts water 1. Wealth luck is exhausted. Strengthen with metal.	**NORTHWEST** 5 8 9 Strong fire 9 as water star, but wealth luck is blocked by earth 5. Use wood to suppress 5 and activate the positive side of 9.
EAST 2 5 3 Hostile wood 3 suppresses wealth luck. Illness star earth 2 is pressed by the earth 3. This is earth sector which strengthens 2. Hang windchimes.	**NORTHEAST** facing palace 7 1 7 Double 7 excellent. Strengthens earth corner. Activate with water for prosperity.	**NORTH** 9 3 5 Unlucky earth 5 as water star is enhanced by fire 9. Suppress with metal & water Use yang water & yang metal.

FRONT OF HOUSE

PERIOD 7 facing SE 1

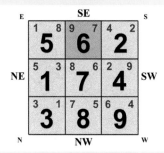

**HOUSE FACING SOUTHEAST 1
PERIOD 7 CHART**

The smaller chart above has been "turned" to bring the Southeast palace to the top. If your house plan is drawn with the entrance at the bottom use the chart on the right. The numbers then correspond to the orientation of Southeast in your plan. Southeast facing houses have the good numbers in the center of the home, with the mountain star 8 placed there. Thus, such homes benefit from a large open floor plan which allows the good Chi of the center of the house to permeate through to the whole house. If the house has a toilet or store room in the center, it means that good luck has been "locked" up. To decide whether or not it is beneficial to change this into a period 8 house depends on how the different rooms in the house have been laid out.

Both of the period charts will have to be analysed before deciding whether or not to change to Period 8.

ANALYSIS OF NUMBERS

WEST	NORTHWEST	NORTH
6 9 4	sitting palace	**3 3 1**
Wood 4 is hurt by metal 6 blocking success in creative fields. Mountain star 6 suggests past luck. Increase children luck with windchimes.	**7 8 5** Unlucky 5 suppresses wealth luck. Metal 7 controls the 5. Strengthen mountain star 7 with lots of metal. Strengthen mountain star.	Water star 1 is auspicious. Place water to activate wealth luck. But wood 3 can exhaust wealth luck. Place fire energy here to suppress mountain 3.

SOUTHWEST	CENTER	NORTHEAST
2 4 9	**- 8 7 6 -**	**5 1 3**
Water star is fire 9. Brings success, but success is blocked & exhausted by earth 2. Mountain star 2 is unlucky for love & family. Suppress 2 with metal.	Mountain star 8 is locked. Earth 8 also exhausted by metal 6. Luck of family, relationships, children & health are blocked. Open areas. Keep well lit.	Water star is wood 3. Unlucky. Mountain star is earth 5, which is also unlucky. The 3 controls the 5. Hang windchimes to suppress wood 3 and exhaust earth 5.

SOUTH	SOUTHEAST	EAST
4 2 2	facing palace	**1 5 8**
Water star is earth 2, an illness star. The wood 4 suppresses the bad star. Activate mountain star 4 in period 7 with plants to bring family luck.	**9 6 7** Water star is lucky this period. Strengthen with water. Fire 9 as mountain star brings good relationship & family luck.	Auspicious water star 8 benefits from real or virtual water. Place large feature here to enhance mountain star water 1.

FRONT OF HOUSE

PERIOD 7 facing SE 2 or 3

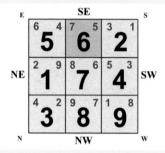

The smaller chart above has been "turned" to bring the Southeast palace to the top. If your house plan is drawn with the entrance at the bottom use the chart on the right. The numbers then correspond to the orientation of Southeast in your plan. In this SE 2/3 facing house, note that the facing palace enjoyed the mountain star 7 through period 7, but come period 8, the 7/5 combination of the facing palace will turn unlucky, bringing loss and burglary.

I would recommend changing this into a period 8 house. However, this also depends on whether the room layout of your house suits a period 7 or a period 8 chart better.

Both of the period charts will have to be analysed before deciding whether or not to change to Period 8.

ANALYSIS OF NUMBERS

WEST	NORTHWEST	NORTH
1 9 8	sitting palace 9 8 7	4 3 2
Auspicious water star 8 benefits from real or virtual water. Place water here. It will aslo enhance mountain star water 1.	Water star lucky this period. Strenthen with water view. Fire 9 as mountain star brings good relationship & family luck.	Water star is earth 2 an illness star. The wood 4 presses the bad star. Activate mountain star 4 in period 7 with plants to bring family luck.
SOUTHWEST	CENTER	NORTHEAST
5 4 3	+ 8 7 6 +	2 1 9
Water star wood 3, unlucky. Mountain star is earth 5, aslo unlucky. 3 controls the 5. Hang windchimes to suppress wood 3 & exhaust earth 5.	Mountain star 8 is locked. Earth 8 also exhausted by metal 6. Luck of family, relationships, children & health are blocked. Open areas. Keep well lit.	Water star is fire 9. Brings success, but success is blocked & exhausted by earth 2. Mountain star 2 is unlucky for love & family. Suppress 2 with metal.
SOUTH	SOUTHEAST	EAST
3 2 1	facing palace 7 6 5	6 5 4
Water star 1 is auspicious. Place water to activate wealth luck. But wood 3 can exhaust wealth luck. Place fire energy to suppress mountain 3.	Unlucky 5 suppresses wealth luck. Metal 7 control the 5. Strengthen mountain star 7 with lots of metal.	Wood 4 is hurt by metal 6 blocking success in creative fields. Mountain star 6 suggests past luck. Increase children luck with windchimes.

FRONT OF HOUSE

PERIOD 7 facing NW 1

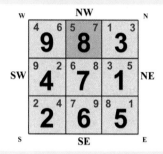

**HOUSE FACING NORTHWEST 1
PERIOD 7 CHART**

The smaller chart above has been "turned" to bring the Northwest palace to the top. If your house plan is drawn with the entrance at the bottom, use the chart on the right. The numbers then correspond to the orientation of Northwest in your plan. In this NW 1 facing house, note that the facing palace enjoyed the water star 7 through period 7, but come period 8, the 5/7 combination of the facing palace will turn very unlucky, bringing loss and illness. The lucky water star in the center makes it difficult to activate the wealth luck of this house in a big way.

I would recommend changing this into a period 8 house.

However, whether the change is beneficial also depends on whether the room layout of your house suits a period 7 or a period 8 chart better. Do remember, however, that all period 7 houses lose energy in the coming new period of 8.

ANALYSIS OF NUMBERS

EAST	SOUTHEAST	SOUTH
8 5 1	sitting palace **7 6 9**	**2 2 4**
Water star 1 brings wealth luck. But it is blocked by earth 8. Better to strengthen lucky mountain star with virtual mountain.	Fire 9 is water star. It brings recognition. The mountain star is lucky metal 7. Strengthen with earth energy - crystals.	Lucky wood 4 is the water star. But it is killed by the earth 2 mountain star. Better to suppress with metal to prevent illness, and family & marriage problems.
NORTHEAST	**CENTER**	**SOUTHWEST**
3 1 5	**- 6 7 8 -**	**9 4 2**
The loss-bringing earth 5 causes loss of wealth. Wood 3 suppresses it, but 3 is also unlucky. Use yin metal to suppress the two numbers.	Water star 8 is locked. Vital to keep spaces open. Enhance with water.. Mountain star metal is strengthened by earth 8. Excellent.	Sickness earth star 2 is the water star. It must be suppressed. But fire 9 strengthens it. Use metal windchime to exhaust 2 & water to control 9.
NORTH	**NORTHWEST**	**WEST**
1 3 3	facing palace **5 8 7**	**4 9 6**
Wood 3 is the water star. It is strengthened by water 1, but it is unlucky. Use fire energy to control 3. As the mountain star 1 is lucky. enhance with yin metal.	Auspicious star is lucky with metal 7. Earth 5 enhances the 7 but as the mountain star, it brings loss & misfortunes.	Metal 6 as the water star signifies past money luck. The wood 4 is good as the mountain star. - enhance it with a small water feature.

FRONT OF HOUSE

PERIOD 7 facing NW 2 or 3

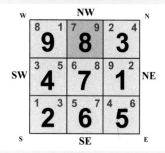

HOUSE FACING NORTHWEST 2/3
PERIOD 7 CHART

The smaller chart has above been "turned" to bring the Northwest palace to the top. If your house plan is drawn with the entrance at the bottom use the chart on the right. The numbers then correspond to the orientation of Northwest in your plan. Note that the NW 1 facing house chart of period 7 is a **Pearl String Chart**. This makes it an especially lucky chart. Also, in this chart, the center length of the house enjoyed good numbers during the period of 7, although the water star 8 being in the center is difficult to energise. I would recommend that although the house enjoys the Pearl String, nevertheless, it is worthwhile thinking about changing this into a period 8 house. This is because of the 7 mountain star in front and the 7 water star at the back. These star numbers occupy important palaces and when the 7 turns ugly in 2004, it could cause problems. **This house should consider changing to period 8 due to the 7's in the front and back palaces.**

94

ANALYSIS OF NUMBERS

EAST	SOUTHEAST	SOUTH
45**6**	sitting palace **5**6**7**	**1**2**3**
Metal 6 is the water star & wood 4 is the mt star. Activate this sector with virtual mountain, such as crystals & stones.	Must have mountain at the back of house to manifest outstanding relationship & health luck. Pearl string transforms the 5.	Water star is 3 & mountain star is water 1. Because of pearl string, activate the mountain star 1 with metal energy & a virtual mountain.

NORTHEAST	CENTER	SOUTHWEST
91**2**	+ **6**7**8** +	**3**4**5**
Sickness earth star 2 is the water star. It must be suppressed. Fire 9 strengthens it. use windchime metal to exhaust 2.	Water star 8 is locked. Vital to have an open floor plan & activate with water for wealth. Metal mountain star is strengthened by earth 8.	Loss bringing earth 5 causes loss of wealth. Wood 3 suppresses it, but 3 is also unlucky. Use yin metal to suppress the two numbers.

NORTH	NORTHWEST	WEST
23**4**	facing palace **7**8**9**	**8**9**1**
Wood 4 is the water star. It is suppressed by earth 2. Use water to enhance the water star aslo pearl string suggests water at front of house.	Must have water in front, because of pearl string. Activate mountain star with metal windchimes.	Water star is auspicious 1 so enhance with water. Mountain star 8 is also excellent. Activate family luck with large crystal cluster.

FRONT OF HOUSE

Analysing
The Period
8 Charts

Chapter 3

Analysing The Period 8 Charts

KEN

THE MOUNTA

The next step in getting the most out of
the change in period is to take a close look
at the Period 8 flying star charts. These charts are
created in accordance with the Flying Star formula for
all periods. However, do note that in every period,
there are charts that are exceptions to the standard
formula. In Period 8, the Southwest and Northeast
facing houses do **not** follow the standard formula of
computation. The charts contained in this book have
been pre-calculated and can be used even by those
who do not know how flying star feng shui charts are
created. The meanings here are summarised to
facilitate easy practice and understanding of Flying
Star feng shui. It certainly cannot be as comprehensive
as taking a proper Master Practitioners Course in
Flying Star feng shui, but it gives the DIY amateur
practitioner a great deal of information to work with.

W hen you familiarise
yourself with Period 8
charts, you will, in actual fact, be
studying the **Chi distribution
of houses** that are built or will
be renovated between February
4th 2004 and February 4th 2024.
This comes in extremely useful
as we move into the new period,
since the Chi distribution map

will enable anyone to identify
the lucky sectors of all **new**
buildings - which include houses,
apartment buildings and offices.

Thus, while one may continue
to live and work inside period
7 buildings (i.e. those which
were built or renovated in the
previous twenty years and

which have not yet been renovated to change to period 8), it is nevertheless useful to know what the luck distribution map will look like should you decide to undertake the renovations required to change the period of your building. As this is almost certain to happen sometime during the twenty years from 2004 through to 2024, these charts will stay relevant for at least 20 years until 2024, as we move into the new period.

You can also compare the sixteen different Period 8 charts that are highlighted in this chapter with the corresponding period 7 charts. Then you will have a basis to select the chart that you feel can best offer you the kind of luck you want. In this context, I want to point out that irrespective of what your personal KUA number may be, you can choose any chart that best corresponds to your land orientation should you be planning to build a new house. You can choose to have

a West group house, even though you may be an East group person under the Eight Mansions formula.

The clever way to practise feng shui is to use flying star period charts to plan the layout of rooms and landscaping, to create water and mountain features that activate the auspicious mountain and water stars of your house, while using Eight Mansions KUA directions to create doors, sitting and sleeping directions that allow each family member to tap their respective best directions.

Thus you can build a Period 8 house that faces, say, a West group direction, and enjoy its good luck, even though you may be an East group person. However, do make certain that you are able to sleep on a bed that allows you to tap your best personal KUA directions, and sit facing your good directions.

The Period 8 Base Chart

The Period 8 base chart has the number 8 as the center number. The other numbers are placed in the direction sectors of the nine-grid chart in a flight pattern that follows the original Lo Shu chart. Thus from 2004 until 2024, the "period numbers" in every sector will each exert their intrinsic influence. The strength of each number's energy is also affected by the sector it occupies. Please note that the base period numbers are also relevant for analysing the luck of sectors in conjunction with the annual and monthly feng shui charts.

In the period of 8, all earth sectors benefit - this means that all Southwest and Northeast houses will be especially auspicious. These two directions form the West group **axis direction** that is reflected in the sequence of the numbers 2, 5 and 8. These numbers make up the very auspicious **parent string number combination**.

This suggests that in the period of 8, all earth sectors offer strong and powerful Chi that brings good fortune.

Do note that the numbers 2 and 5 are the traditional **affliction** numbers according to Flying Star analysis. They bring loss of health and finances. So note how they get strengthened in the NE and SW sectors where they appear as period numbers. But 8 in the center combines with the 2/5 to make the parent string. This suggests that there are hidden treasures in the earth numbers. So SW and NE facing numbers have nothing to fear from the 2/5 in the center of their charts.

The number 8 is also an earth number, and in its period, it rules the earth numbers. Thus 8 supercedes and controls the negative influences of 2 and 5. As your knowledge of Flying Star deepens, you will begin to appreciate the enormous power of the earth numbers, for bringing good as well as bad luck.

PERIOD 8 BASE CHART NUMBERS

ANALYSING based on the FIVE ELEMENTS

7 METAL into WOOD	**3** WOOD into FIRE	**5** EARTH into EARTH
DESTRUCTIVE	PRODUCTIVE	AFFINITY
# 7 brings danger.	# 3 enhances reputation.	Earth gets strengthened.
SOUTHEAST	**SOUTH**	**SOUTHWEST**
6 METAL into WOOD	**8** EARTH into EARTH	**1** WATER into METAL
DESTRUCTIVE	Mountain has silent strength & hidden treasures. Young men rise.	EXHAUSTING
but 6 is not as harmful.		# 1 causes Chi to weaken
EAST		**WEST**
2 EARTH into EARTH	**4** WOOD into WATER	**9** FIRE into METAL
AFFINITY	EXHAUSTING	DESTRUCTIVE
Earth gets strengthened.	# 4 causes Chi to weaken.	Fire at Heaven's Gate.
NORTHEAST	**NORTH**	**NORTHWEST**

PERIOD 8 facing SOUTH 1

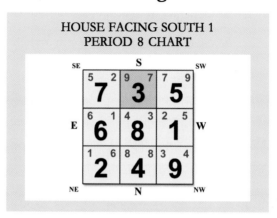

HOUSE FACING SOUTH 1
PERIOD 8 CHART

The SOUTH 1 facing house enjoys the auspicious double 8 in its sitting palace. So it can be interpreted as a lucky house. This house would benefit from a mountain feature placed in the Northeast sector of the property. If the back of the house is higher, it automatically activates the mountain star 8, bringing beneficial relationships and good health to residents.

Inside the home, place a bubbling water bowl (with or without fish) in the North corner of the living room. This will activate the water star 8 of the living room, thereby attracting income and wealth luck into the house. Study the analysis of water and mountain stars of the different sectors of the house summarised in the chart on the right.

ANALYSIS OF NUMBERS

SOUTHEAST 5 7 2	SOUTH facing palace 9 3 7	SOUTHWEST 7 5 9
Misfortunes & extreme bad luck. Illness, money loss and accidents. Be careful when monthly & annual 2 or 5 enters. Use windchimes or build storeroom.	Problems from flirtations & fire hazard. Can become scandalous. Use yin water cure to control the 7 & subdue the 9.	Extreme problems. All troubles caused by excessive vulnerability to sexual advances. Danger of fire hazards. Use yin water or big earth boulders to suppress.
EAST 6 6 1	CENTER 4 8 3	WEST 2 1 5
Peach blossom luck! Amazing financial luck for high achievers. Use metal chimes, coins and bells to capture the benefit. **VERY AUSPICIOUS!**	Double wood element destroys family harmony. Emotional stress due to relationship problems. Marriage & sibling discontent. Use bright lights here.	Extremely dangerous for health. Total financial loss. Bad when annual or monthly 5 flies in - sudden illness or accident. Use moving metal energy - clocks, fans, windchimes.
NORTHEAST 1 2 6	NORTH 8 4 8	NORTHWEST 3 9 4
Amazing 1/6 Ho Tu combination brings luck for scholastic intelligence for entrepreneural skills. Very good for 2nd son. Use chimes & bells to capture luck.	Excellent combination for plentiful wealth, health & prosperity. Build a mountain feature here to benefit. Best place for bedroom. **VERY AUSPICIOUS!**	Wood clashes with metal sector. Danger of mental instability. Theft indicated. Mature women and patriarch stressed out. Use quiet metal objects like coins and metal swords.

PERIOD 8 facing SOUTH 2/3

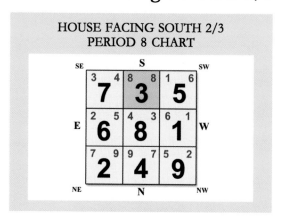

HOUSE FACING SOUTH 2/3 PERIOD 8 CHART

The SOUTH 2/3 facing house enjoys the auspicious double 8 in its facing palace. This means that the front door should be located in the middle sector of the front part of the house as the door is a powerful activator of the double 8.

I also suggest placing an impressive water feature in the Southwest part of the house as this activates the **indirect spirit** of the house, which brings wealth luck. The problem is that water on the right of the main door causes the patriarch to develop a roving eye. To overcome this, place an amethyst geode tied with red string under the matriarchal bed. Study the analysis of water and mountain stars of the different sectors of the house summarised in the chart on the right.

ANALYSIS OF NUMBERS

SOUTHEAST **374**	**SOUTH** facing palace **838**	**SOUTHWEST** **156**
Eldest daughter's luck afflicted with stress. Some scholastic success, but misunderstandings bring severe mental stress. **MENTAL PROBLEMS**	Double 8 here brings good fortune to household. Benefits from large hall/foyer. **VERY AUSPICIOUS!**	Benefits working mothers. Women have success. Businesses & careers bring financial gain. Enhance with crytals. Wear jewellery. **VERY AUSPICIOUS!**
EAST **265**	**CENTER** **483**	**WEST** **611**
Serious & extreme bad luck. Illness luck. Danger of loss of money, especially for eldest son. Build a store room to lock up stars or use windchimes.	Double wood destroys family harmony. Emotional stress due to relationship problems. Marriage & sibling discontentment. Use bright lights to exhaust wood.	Amazing financial luck for high achievers! Benefits descendants. Use metal chimes, coins & bells to capture benefit! **PEACH BLOSSOM LUCK!**
NORTHEAST **729**	**NORTH** **947**	**NORTHWEST** **592**
Extreme problems and troubles caused by vulnerability to sexual advances. Danger of fire hazards. Use yin water or earth boulders to suppress.	Problems from flirtations & fire hazard. Can become scandalous. Use yin water cure to control 7 and defuse 9. **MISFORTUNE LUCK**	Misfortunes & extreme bad luck from illness & loss. Patriarch vulnerable when 5 and 2 flies in. Use windchimes or build a store room to trap bad stars.

PERIOD 8 facing NORTH 1

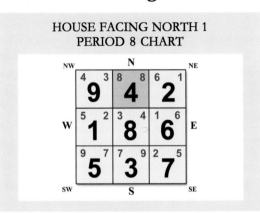

HOUSE FACING NORTH 1
PERIOD 8 CHART

The NORTH 1 facing house enjoys the auspicious double 8 in its facing palace. So it can be interpreted as a lucky house. This house benefits if the main door is located in the North sector to activate the double 8 combination. This house benefits those in the communication professions, because the period star 4 brings that sort of luck.

Place a bubbling water bowl (with or without fish) in the North corner of the living room. This will activate the water star 8, thereby attracting income and wealth luck into the house. Make sure poison arrows inside the room do not afflict it. Study the analysis of water and mountain stars of the different sectors of the house summarised in the chart on the right.

ANALYSIS OF NUMBERS

NORTHWEST	NORTH	NORTHEAST
4 9 3	facing palace **8 4 8**	**6 2 1**
Emotional problems. Marital discord. Women take their toll. Father under stress.	Double 8 brings good fortune to household. Water feature here will attract money luck.	Good career luck. High achievers get success. Financial abundance can be activated with coins & crystals.
STRESS AFFLICTIONS	**VERY AUSPICIOUS!**	**PEACH BLOSSOM LUCK!**
WEST	CENTER	EAST
5 1 2	**3 8 4**	**1 6 6**
Extreme bad luck. Misfortunes bring loss & ill health. Need to be careful.	Wood stars in center exhaust residents. Quarrelsome 3 brings disharmony & discord. Display crystal balls to restore peace & harmony.	This sector good for men. Scholastic success. Money comes from metal. Activate with chimes & coins.
ILLNESS STARS		**AUSPICIOUS FOR SONS**
SOUTHWEST	SOUTH	SOUTHEAST
9 5 7	**7 3 9**	**2 7 5**
Innocent flirtations turn nasty & hurtful. Danger of scandals. Vulnerability of women. Violence & blackmail.	Extreme problems in Period of 8. Must control with water, which exhausts 7 & extinguishes 9. Violence & fire.	Situation of total loss. Dangerous combination. Prone to sudden accidents. Must control with metal windchimes.
SEXUAL PROBLEMS	**YIN WATER CURE**	**DANGER TO HEALTH**

PERIOD 8 facing NORTH 2/3

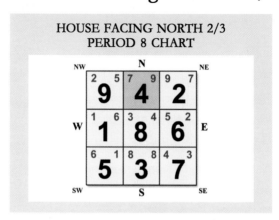

In a NORTH 2/3 facing house the auspicious double 8 combination flies to the sitting palace of the house. This indicates a lucky house BUT the kitchen must not be located in the South sector, as this could kill the double 8. Take note of this in the layout arrangements of your home. Also note that all three sectors of the front part of the house do not have auspicious numbers. The 2/5 and 9/7 combinations bring illness, loss and burglaries. From the analysis of water and mountain star numbers in the different sectors of the house in the summary chart, you will see that it is best to locate a main door in the South sector at teh back of the house. In this house, all good luck emanates from the South.

It is a good idea to place the living room at the back of the house and to have a garden located behind the house.

ANALYSIS OF NUMBERS

NORTHWEST	NORTH	NORTHEAST
2 9 5	facing palace **7 4 9**	**9 2 7**
Total loss scenario. Danger of stroke & terminal illness. Loss of vitality. Control with 6 rod metal windchime. **DANGEROUS**	Afflicted facing palace. Threat of violence. Burglary & loss. Bad in period of 8. **MISFORTUNE LUCK**	Research & studies cannot succeed. Danger of scandals. Vulnerability of sons. Violence & blackmail. **DANGER OF LOSS**
WEST **1 1 6**	CENTER **3 8 4**	EAST **5 6 2**
Sector benefits 2nd son. Scholastic honours. Intelligence is enhanced, bringing good exam results. Heaven luck brings good finances.	Wood stars in center exhaust residents. Quarrelsome 3 brings disharmony. Three crystal balls here will bring peace & harmony.	Extreme bad luck. Misfortunes bring loss & ill health. Need to be careful. **ILLNESS STARS**
SOUTHWEST **6 5 1**	SOUTH **8 3 8**	SOUTHEAST **4 7 3**
Good career luck. Networking brings financial gains. Crystals activate your blossoming. **PEACH BLOSSOM LUCK!**	Double 8 gives excellent support in sitting palace. Spend time at the back of the house. Activate mountain star with a concrete wall.	Emotion problems. Marital discord. Women take their toll. Eldest son will be very pressured. **STRESS AFFLICTIONS**

PERIOD 8 facing EAST 1

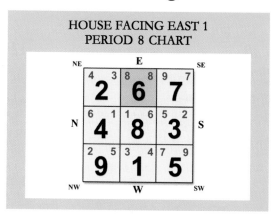

In an EAST 1 facing house, the auspicious double 8 combination flies to the facing palace of the house. It is thus beneficial to locate the main door in the middle part of the front of the house to activate the lucky mountain and water stars. Meanwhile, the center numbers of East facing houses make up the lucky 1/6/8 combination. Such houses benefit from an open-space concept in the living area. As the surrounding numbers are not lucky combinations (apart from North, which has the 6/1 combination) it is advisable to make the center room as large and as open as possible. Do not locate toilets, kitchens and storerooms here.

Study the analysis of water and mountain stars of the different sectors of the house summarised in the chart on the right.

ANALYSIS OF NUMBERS

NORTHEAST	EAST	SOUTHEAST
4 2 3	facing palace	9 7 7
Relationship problems. Marriage problems. Financial partnerships will turn hostile. Wood into earth can cause problems.	8 6 8 — Double 8 brings good fortune. Activate water 8 for wealth & mountain 8 for health. Locate door here. **AUSPICIOUS SECTOR!**	Danger of burglary. Violence hurts daughters. Problems with eyes & heart. Loss of income through betrayal. **LOSS THROUGH ROBBERY**

NORTH	CENTER	SOUTH
6 4 1	1 8 6	5 3 2
Peach blossom luck! Career luck improves. Relationship luck can be enhanced with metal chimes & bells. Do not place water here. **AUSPICIOUS SECTOR**	Concentration of white numbers bring good fortune for family. Wealth luck for patriarch. Marriage & relationships enjoy good luck. **PROTECT THE CENTER**	Misfortunes & extreme bad luck. Illness luck. Sickness is fatal. Best not to occupy this sector. **DANGEROUS**

NORTHWEST	WEST	SOUTHWEST
2 9 5	Sitting Palace	7 5 9
Danger to health. Total loss financially. Accidents & mishaps. Patriarch is threatened. Dangerous when annual and month 5/2 flies in. **DANGEROUS**	3 1 4 — Mental problems. Misunderstandings. Hostility & bad health. Very stressful situations. Luck for young girls **STRESSED OUT**	Severe problems. 7 is very dangerous here. Danger of fire hazards. Beware of predatory females. Ward off third party threats with yin water. **DANGEROUS**

PERIOD 8 facing EAST 2/3

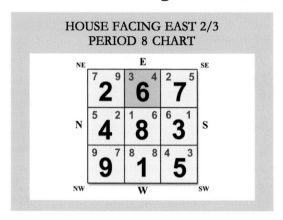

HOUSE FACING EAST 2/3
PERIOD 8 CHART

In an EAST 2/3 facing house, the auspicious double 8 combination flies to the back and occupies the sitting palace of the house. This suggests the potential for locating the living room and activity area at the back of the house. Whenever you have the auspicious double 8 combination, it always represents good feng shui when the house is designed to activate these numbers. The best is to have it be the busiest part of the house.

All East-facing houses have the auspicious 1/6/8 combination in the center. Such houses benefit from the open space concept in the center. Do not locate toilets, kitchens and storerooms here. Study the analysis of water and mountain stars of the different sectors of the house summarised in the chart on the right.

ANALYSIS OF NUMBERS

NORTHEAST 7 2 9	EAST facing palace 3 6 4	SOUTHEAST 2 7 5
Unlucky star combination causes severe problems. Danger of fire accidents. Burglary & violence. 7 is dangerous. **BE CAREFUL**	Mental problems. Misunderstandings. Hostility & bad health. Stressful situations. Luck for young girls. **RELATIONSHIP PROBLEMS**	Dangerous to health. Total loss financially. Accidents & mishaps. Daughter threatened. Dangerous when annual & month 5/2 flies in. **DANGEROUS**
NORTH 5 4 2	CENTER 1 8 6	SOUTH 6 3 1
Misfortunes & extreme bad luck. Illness luck. Sickness is fatal. Best not to occupy this sector. **ILLNESS STARS**	Concentration of white numbers bring great good fortune for family. Wealth luck for patriarch. Create open room concept for center of the house.	Peach blossom luck. Career luck improves when sector has water. Relationship luck can be enhanced with metal chimes & bells. **GOOD FOR CAREER**
NORTHWEST 9 9 7	WEST Sitting Palace 8 1 8	SOUTHWEST 4 5 3
Financial loss. Danger to patriarch. 9 causes heart problems. Partners & friends may betray you. Control with yin water. **DANGER TO FATHER**	Double 8 brings good fortune. Activate water 8 for wealth & mountain 8 for health. Locate back door here. **AUSPICIOUS SECTOR**	Marriage problems. Financial partnerships will turn hostile. Wood into earth causes problems in finances and relationships.

PERIOD 8 facing WEST 1

HOUSE FACING WEST 1
PERIOD 8 CHART

In a WEST 1 facing house, the auspicious double 8 combination flies to the sitting palace of the house. This suggests the main area of activity of the household should be at the back of the house. Locating the living area here would make good feng shui sense. All three of the front sectors have troublesome afflicted star numbers. If possible, place the main door in the North sector. Meanwhile, take advantage of the auspicious 1/6/8 combination in the center by having a large open space concept there. If you have a living cum dining area here extending into the East sector where the double 8 is located, you would be making fullest use of the period 8 chart. Do not locate toilets, kitchens and storerooms here. Study the analysis of water and mountain stars of the different sectors of the house summarised in the chart on the right.

ANALYSIS OF NUMBERS

SOUTHWEST 9 5 7	WEST facing palace 4 1 3	NORTHWEST 5 9 2
Problems arising from extreme flirtatious tendencies. Cheating which leads to money loss. Use yin water to control both 9 and 7 stars.	Emotional & mental stress due to relationship problems caused by double wood. Children vulnerable. Use earth colour scheme.	Dangerous stars of illness & wealth loss. Health problems. Financial loss severe for patriarch. Use windchimes or moving metal. Do not live here.
SOUTH 2 3 5	CENTER 6 8 1	NORTH 1 4 6
Such dangerous stars of illness & loss. Reputation tarnished. Use windchimes & yin water to cure. Do not place kitchen in this sector.	Most auspicious stars! Activate with water or keep as open space. Good for bedroom. Wasted if bathroom is here. **AUSPICIOUS SECTOR!**	Amazing financial luck for high achievers. Use metal windchimes. Use coins & bells to capture luck. **PEACH BLOSSOM LUCK!**
SOUTHEAST 7 7 9	EAST Sitting Palace 8 6 8	NORTHEAST 3 2 4
Extreme problems caused by vulnerability to sexual advances & problems. Fire hazard. Use water to fight excessive fire energy.	Extremely auspicious luck for wealth, health & popularity. Definitely place your back door here to capture double 8 stars.	Danger of mental instability or stress for mature women of the house. Children studying also affected. Double wood saps earth. Place bright lights. **MENTAL STRESS**

PERIOD 8 facing WEST 2/3

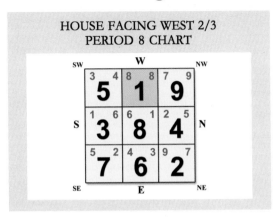

HOUSE FACING WEST 2/3
PERIOD 8 CHART

In a WEST 2/3 facing house, the auspicious double 8 combination flies to the front and occupies the facing palace of the house. This suggests the main door should be located in the front center, to activate and energise the double 8 here. It is also a very good idea to build a water feature in the Southwest of the garden if you can, to tap the indirect spirit of the period. This brings big money luck to the home. Meanwhile, the center sector of West-facing houses has the auspicious 1/8/6 combination. Such houses benefit from the large open-space concept in the living area. It is beneficial to make the center of the house as large as possible. Do not locate toilets, kitchens and storerooms here. Study the analysis of the water and mountain star numbers of the different sectors of the house in the chart on the right to familiarise yourself with the combination star numbers for your house.

ANALYSIS OF NUMBERS

SOUTHWEST 3 5 4 Danger of mental instability or stress, especially for matriarch. Double wood saps earth energy. Place bright lights to counter.	**WEST** facing palace 8 1 8 Extremely fantastic luck for wealth, health & popularity. Place main door here. Double 8 star benefits the whole family!	**NORTHWEST** 7 9 9 Extreme problems caused by vulnerability to sexual advances & problems. Patriarch vulnerable. Use water to fight excessive fire. Do not place kitchen here.
SOUTH 1 3 6 Amazing financial luck for high achievers. Use metal chimes, coins & bells to capture the benefit. **PEACH BLOSSOM LUCK!**	**CENTER** 6 8 1 Most auspicious combination of stars. Activate with water & keep as an open space. Good for bedroom. Wasted if bathroom is located here.	**NORTH** 2 4 5 Dangerous stars of illness & loss. Health problems. Career is harmed. Use lots of windchimes & moving metal energy to combat the bad stars. Do not live here.
SOUTHEAST 5 7 2 Dangerous illness & wealth loss stars. Health problems. Financial loss is severe. Use lots of windchimes or bells to fight 2 and 5.	**EAST** Sitting Palace 4 6 3 Emotional & mental stress due to relationship problems. Sons are vulnerable. Use red colour scheme to exhaust wood.	**NORTHEAST** 9 2 7 Problems arise from extreme flirtatious tendencies. Cheating resulting in money loss. Use yin water.

PERIOD 8 facing SW 1

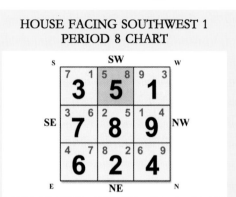

All SOUTHWEST facing houses enjoy exceptional good fortune in the Period of 8. When the facing direction is Southwest 1, the house enjoys the **sum-of-ten** combination with the period and mountain stars combining. This brings exceptional relationship, networking and health luck.

The center number combination is the very auspicious earth string 2/8/5 combination. Such houses will therefore also benefit from having a large open space concept throughout the house. To make the most of the special sum-of-ten numbers, try to make the shape of your house as regular (i.e. square or rectangle) as possible. This maximises the powerful sum-of-ten effect.

ANALYSIS OF NUMBERS - SUM-OF-TEN

SOUTH	SOUTHWEST	WEST
731	facing palace **558**	**913**
Turns nasty in Period 8. Wealth loss & metal related injuries. Use yang water to drown 7 & activate water 1.	Limbs, joints & bones have problems. Danger of paralysis. Be careful of rough sports. Place water feature to capture prosperity.	Legal problems & disputes, but help comes from good relationships. Do not use noisy metal here. **QUARRELSOME LUCK**
SOUTHEAST	CENTER	NORTHWEST
376	**285**	**194**
Period of slow growth Limbs have problems. Danger of accidents. Use yin water to overcome problems. **MISFORTUNE LUCK**	Severe loss & illness. Extremely dangerous to health & total loss financially. Build a storeroom to lock stars or use moving metal.	Political luck & media attention. Lots of romance luck. Use slow moving water or plants to enhance good luck. **MEDIA ATTENTION**
EAST	NORTHEAST	NORTH
467	Sitting Palace **822**	**649**
Bad luck in love. Danger of being cheated or taken for a ride by opposite sex. Miscarriage. Use yang water to remedy.	Good mountain 8 star, but bad water star. Use mountain principle to enhance. Be careful when 2 or 5 flies in.	Fire at heaven's gate. Danger of fire & arguments. Must not have kitchen here. Use yin water cure. **FIRE HAZARD**

PERIOD 8 facing SW 2/3

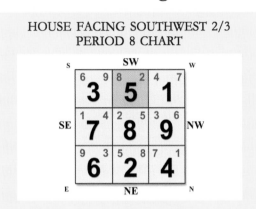

HOUSE FACING SOUTHWEST 2/3 PERIOD 8 CHART

All SOUTHWEST facing houses enjoy exceptional good fortune in the Period of 8. When the facing direction is Southwest 2/3, the house enjoys the **Parent String** combination of numbers. This is regarded as exceptionally auspicious and the house is said to have the potential of enjoying exceptional luck in all areas, including relationship and money luck. More, the luck is said to carry through to three generations.

The center number combination is the very auspicious earth string 2/8/5 combination. Such houses will therefore also benefit from having a large open space concept throughout the house.

ANALYSIS OF NUMBERS - PARENT STRING

SOUTH 6**3**9	SOUTHWEST facing palace 8**5**2	WEST 4**1**7
Fire at heaven's gate. Arguments & fire hazard. Must not have kitchen here. Use yin water cure by using big containers of water.	Auspicious mountain 8 star but bad water star. Use crystals to enhance the good mountain star, but weaken the water 2 with windchimes.	Bad luck in love. Will get cheated or taken for a ride by the opposite sex. Miscarriage. Use yang water to remedy. Use the colour blue.
SOUTHEAST 1**7**4	CENTER 2**8**5	NORTHWEST 3**9**6
Political & media attention. Lots of romance for women and men. Use slow moving water or plants to enhance good luck.	Very bad luck indeed Loss $ illness. Extremely dangerous to health & wealth. Build storeroom or use moving metal - (e.g. clocks, windchimes, fans).	Period of slow growth. Limbs have problems. Danger of accidents. Use yin water to overcome the problem. **MISFORTUNE LUCK**
EAST 9**6**3	NORTHEAST Sitting Palace 5**2**8	NORTH 7**4**1
Legal problems & disputes, but help comes from good relationships. Use lights to enhance 9 & exhaust problematic 3. Do not use noisy metal.	Limb, joint & bone problems. Danger of paralysis. Be careful of rough sports. Use water feature to capture prosperity.	Extreme bad luck in Period 8. Wealth loss & metal-related injuries. Use yang water to drown the lethal 7 star. **CAN BE DANGEROUS**

PERIOD 8 facing NE 1

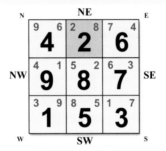

HOUSE FACING NORTHEAST 1
PERIOD 8 CHART

All NORTHEAST facing houses enjoy exceptional good fortune in the Period of 8. When the facing direction is Northeast 1, the house enjoys the **sum-of-ten** combination with the period and mountain stars combining. This brings exceptional relationship, networking and health luck.

The center number combination is the auspicious earth string 2/8/5 combination. Such houses will therefore also benefit from having a large open space concept throughout the house. To make the most of the special sum-of-ten numbers, try to make the shape of your house as regular (i.e. square or rectangle) as possible, as this will maximise the sum-of-ten effect.

ANALYSIS OF NUMBERS - SUM-OF-TEN

NORTH	NORTHEAST	EAST
9**4**6	facing palace	7**6**4
	2**2**8	
Fire at heaven's gate subdued by water in the north. Can bring career problems. Use yin water & hang windchimes.	Riches & wealth, but plenty of illness. Excellent water star brings wealth. Place yang water to capture wealth & drown illness star.	Taken for a ride by someone of the opposite sex. Cheating of partner in romance, especially for son. Install lights.
AVERAGE LUCK		**BE CAREFUL**
NORTHWEST	CENTER	SOUTHEAST
4**9**1	5**8**2	6**7**3
Romance luck, but too much water leads to sex scandals & affairs, leading to unhappiness & break-up of family. Enhance with plants & small water for wealth.	Loss stars in the center of home brings problems to everyone. Misfortunes & extreme bad luck. Build a storeroom to lock up bad stars.	Unexpected friendships. Danger of betrayal for patriarch. Danger of car accidents. Be careful. Balance with crystal gemstones.
WEST	SOUTHWEST	SOUTH
3**1**9	Sitting Palace	1**3**7
	8**5**5	
Youngest daughter tends to become rebellious, but is subdued by the fiery 9. Do not place water here.	Danger or paralysis and illness of serious nature. Mountain star 8 very auspicious. Strengthen with large natural crystal.	Robbery & loss of wealth indicated. Place protective symbols. Suppress with yin water & lights.
NOT SO AUSPICIOUS		**DANGEROUS**

PERIOD 8 facing NE 2/3

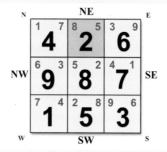

**HOUSE FACING NORTHEAST 2/3
PERIOD 8 CHART**

All NORTHEAST facing houses enjoy exceptional good fortune in the Period of 8. When the facing direction is Northeast 2/3, the house enjoys the **Parent String** combination, which brings exceptional all round money and relationship luck.

The center number combination is the auspicious earth string 2/8/5 combination. Such houses will therefore also benefit from having a large open space concept throughout the house. To make the most of the special parent string numbers, try to make the shape of your house as regular (i.e. square or rectangle) as possible. This will maximise the good effect of the parent string combination.

ANALYSIS OF NUMBERS - PARENT STRING

NORTH 1**4**7	NORTHEAST facing palace 8**2**5	EAST 3**6**9
Loss of wealth - could be due to nasty metal 7 star. Place yin water here. **DANGEROUS**	Danger or paralysis & serious illness. Mountain star 8 auspicious. Strengthen with large crystal. Suppress 5 with windchime.	Quarrelsome mountain star, but subdued by the 9. Do not do anything further to this sector. Son will have average luck. **MEDIOCRE LUCK**
NORTHWEST 6**9**3	CENTER 5**8**2	SOUTHEAST 4**7**1
Unexpected friendships. Danger of betrayal for the patriarch. Danger of car accidents. Be careful. Balance with crystal gemstones.	Loss of stars in the center of the home brings problems to everyone. Misfortunes & extreme bad luck. Lock up stars in storeroom.	Romance luck, but too much water leads to sex scandals & affairs, leading to family break-up. Enhance with plants & small water for wealth.
WEST 7**1**4	SOUTHWEST Sitting Palace 2**5**8	SOUTH 9**3**6
Taken for a ride by someone of the opposite sex or cheating of partner in a romance, especially for youngest daughter. Install lights.	Richness & wealth, but there is illness. Excellent water star brings wealth! Place water to harness wealth & drown illness. Powerful matriarch.	Fire at heaven's gate made worse by the fiery South. Gossip & slander problems. Dangerous for patriarch. Avoid having kitchen here. Place protection. Use yin water.

PERIOD 8 facing SE 1

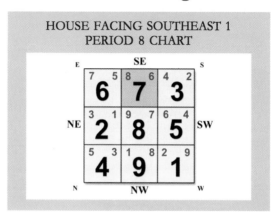

**HOUSE FACING SOUTHEAST 1
PERIOD 8 CHART**

A SOUTHEAST 1 facing house enjoys sequential numbers in all the sectors and this is often referred to as the **Pearl String** combination. This is a very lucky facing direction and the house brings exceptional relationships and networking luck when the main door also faces the same direction and is located in the Southeast sector. Placing water at the back of the house will benefit the residents. The luckiest sectors of the house are the center sectors. Thus, store rooms and kitchens are best located at the two sides of the house. Study the detailed analysis of the water and mountain star numbers of the different sectors of the house in the summary chart to the right to familiarise yourself with the combination star numbers for your house.

ANALYSIS OF NUMBERS

EAST	SOUTHEAST	SOUTH
765	facing palace 876	432
Mouth related problems. Arguments leading to emotional stress. Not so good for son. Stress & afflictions.	Most auspicious for health & relationships. Popularity & recognition enters main door. Use crystals to enhance.	Illness & internal organ problems. Husband has affairs. Mother-in-law causes problems. Use water to reduce stress. **STRESSFUL LUCK**
NORTHEAST	CENTER	SOUTHWEST
321	987	654
Prosperity brought by water star 1. Great for study or home office. Use yang water to activate. Plant bamboo grove here. **VERY GOOD LUCK**	Problems arise from extreme flirtatious tendency. Fire hazard. 7 star brings misfortune Use yin water to control. **MISFORTUNE LUCK**	Surprise windfall for women & excellent romance luck! Matriarch benefits enormously. Enhance with windchimes & crystals. Use dragon image.
NORTH	NORTHWEST	WEST
543	Sitting Palace 198	219
Money troubles. Disputes & bad business luck. Could be damaging to careers. Bad for sons. Use yin water to disarm mountain 5 & control quarrels.	Fantastic water star 8! Excellent prosperity Use yang water feature. Great as office or bedroom of breadwinner.	Peach blossom luck for women. Romance does not last. Nothing succeeds unless remedied. Use water plants to correct. **PEACH BLOSSOM LUCK!**

PERIOD 8 facing SE 2/3

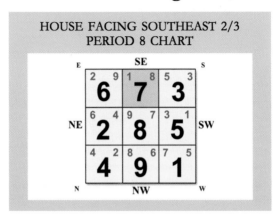

HOUSE FACING SOUTHEAST 2/3 PERIOD 8 CHART

A SOUTHEAST 2/3 facing house has the auspicious water star 8 at the front of the house. When the main door is placed here, it will activate wealth luck for the residents. The combination of numbers in many of other sectors is, however, not terribly lucky, and it is necessary to disarm or control some of the afflicted sectors.

The back of the house will benefit from a mountain-type feature such as a high wall, or if there is a taller building behind which will provide support. Study the detailed chart to the right to examine the Chi distribution in each of the sectors of the house. Note that this house benefits from having water at the front of the house.

ANALYSIS OF NUMBERS

EAST	SOUTHEAST	SOUTH
2 6 9	facing palace **1 7 8**	**5 3 3**
Peach blossom luck for women. Romance does not last. Nothing succeeds unless corrected with water plants. **PEACH BLOSSOM LUCK!**	Fantastic water 8 star. Excellent prosperity luck. Use yang water feature. Great as entrance & bedroom of breadwinner.	Money troubles. Disputes & bad business luck. Bad for sons. Use yin water to disarm mountain 5 & control quarrels by 3 star. Reputation may suffer.
NORTHEAST **6 2 4**	CENTER **9 8 7**	SOUTHWEST **3 5 1**
Unexpected windfall for women & excellent romance luck. Matriarch benefits. Enhance with crystals & use dragon image.	Problems arise from extreme flirtatious tendency. Fire hazard 7 star brings misfortune. Use yin water to control 7 and weaken 9.	Prosperity brought by wonderful water star 1. Use yang water to activate. Matriarch benefits. **VERY GOOD LUCK**
NORTH **4 4 2**	NORTHWEST Sitting Palace **8 9 6**	WEST **7 1 5**
Clash of wood & earth. Illness & internal organ problems. Husband has affairs. Mother-in-law causes problems. Use water. **STRESSFUL LUCK**	Most auspicious for health & relationships. Popularity & recognition enters through backdoor. Use boulders to enhance.	Mouth-related problems. Arguments leading to emotional stress. Not so good for sons. **STRESSFUL LUCK**

PERIOD 8 facing NW 1

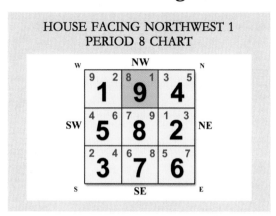

A NORTHWEST 1 facing house enjoys the powerful **Pearl String** combination as well as a very auspicious mountain star at the front. Here, the mountain star 8 brings stunning networking and mentor luck. Make sure your main door is placed in this Northwest sector.

The back of the house will benefit from a water feature, but make sure there is a door there to receive the benefits, otherwise there will be missed opportunities. Study the detailed analysis of numbers in the chart on the right to familiarise yourself with the combination star numbers for your house. This house benefits from a water feature at the back.

ANALYSIS OF NUMBERS - PEARL STRING

WEST	NORTHWEST	NORTH
91**2**	facing palace **8**9**1**	**3**4**5**
Problems with children, but good relationship luck, especially for youngest daughter. Use metal to control illness star 2.	Superb combination of stars! Mountain 8 brings auspicious relationships & health. Plenty of money. Do not use water. Place crystals to benefit.	Loss of wealth. Severe cash flow problems. Financial loss is severe. If kitchen is here, sickness is inevitable. Use copper mountain painting to fight. **DANGEROUS**
SOUTHWEST	CENTER	NORTHEAST
45**6**	**7**8**9**	**1**2**3**
Woman of the house will bear heavy burden. Strengthen earth element with crystals. Use water to strengthen the water star 6.	Loss stars in the center of home brings problems to everyone. Misfortunes & extreme bad luck. Look up stars with storeroom. **DANGEROUS**	Wealth & fame luck, but gossip & lawsuits cause aggravation. Use water plants to enhance & use still water to diffuse misunderstandings.
SOUTH	SOUTHEAST	EAST
23**4**	Sitting Palace **6**7**8**	**5**6**7**
Wives & mother-in-laws quarrel & fight. Clashing of wood & earth causes disharmony in love or marriage. Subdue mountain 2 with green plants.	Superb combination of stars! Money, popularity & prosperity from backdoor. Place yang water feature to activate. **AUSPICIOUS!**	Danger caused by excessive gossiping. Danger of mouth-related problems. Robbery or injury to limbs in Period 8. Use metal & plants to combat bad stars.

PERIOD 8 facing NW 2/3

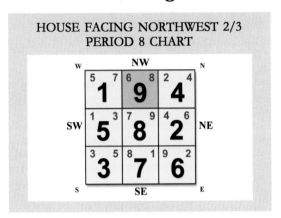

HOUSE FACING NORTHWEST 2/3
PERIOD 8 CHART

A NORTHWEST 2/3 facing house enjoys an excellent water star in front. Note that compared to a NW 1 house, the water star 8 has flipped to the front of the house, while the mountain star 8 has gone to the back. Thus it benefits from a water feature in the front.

This house has one of the lesser attractive combination of star numbers as most of the other sectors have sickness star afflictions. However, if the focus of feng shui can be directed to the front and back of the house, residents can enjoy tremendous good fortune.

Study the chart to the right for a detailed analysis of the combination of numbers in each of the sectors.

ANALYSIS OF NUMBERS

WEST	NORTHWEST	NORTH
51**7**	facing palace	**2**4**4**
Danger cause by excessive gossiping. Danger of mouth-related problems. Robbery and injury to limbs in Period 8. Use metal and plants. **DANGEROUS**	**6**9**8** Superb combination of white stars. Money popularity & prosperity luck from the main door. Place yang water feature to activate.	Wives and mother-in-laws quarrel and fight. Disharmony in love or marriage. Subdue mountain 2 star with green plants, which also strengthens romantic 4.
SOUTHWEST	CENTER	NORTHEAST
15**3**	**7**8**9**	**4**2**6**
Wealth & fame luck, but lawsuits & gossip cause aggravation. Use water plants to enhance and yin water to diffuse misunderstandings caused by water star 3.	Loss stars in the center brings problems. Misfortunes & extreme bad luck. Build storeroom to lock up the bad stars. **DANGEROUS**	Women of the house will bear heavy burden. Strengthen earth element with crystals. Use water to strengthen water star 6. **STRESS AFFLICTION**
SOUTH	SOUTHEAST	EAST
33**5**	Sitting Palace	**9**6**2**
Loss of wealth. Severe cash flow problems. Financial loss. If kitchen is here, illness is inevitable. Use copper mountain painting to fight 5. Avoid staying here.	**8**7**1** Superb combination. Mountain star 8 brings health & relationship luck. Plenty of money. Do not use water. Place earth boulders here.	Problems with children, but good relationship luck, especially for the son. Use metal & plants to control illness star 2.

Comparing Period 7 & 8 Natal Charts

Chapter 4

Comparing The Charts

Once you have familiarised yourself with both the Period 7 and Period 8 charts, the next step is to take a close look at how each of these charts affect the luck distribution of your home. Note that all SW and NE oriented houses benefit from exceptionally good number combinations in the Period of 8, so all SW or NE facing houses and buildings should change.

But not everyone can or need to opt for this orientation. For instance, if your house is already facing a field (auspicious bright hall) as shown here,  you might not wish to change; and if facing an auspicious direction means having to face a poison arrow, it might be better to avoid the poison arrow effect. In practising Flying Star feng shui, we **cannot** ignore the physical environment. We must understand and accept that an auspicious orientation can often be made inauspicious by surrounding landforms.

I t is necessary to examine the luck of each sector based on the layout plan and flow of Chi in your house. Sometimes you may have a basically lucky chart, but if all the lucky numbers are "locked up" by storerooms and bathrooms being located smack in the auspicious number sectors, you will not benefit from the good luck.

Other times, it may be that your bedroom has been laid out to

occupy the unluckiest of sectors. So just by having a lucky facing direction for the period does not always guarantee a lucky house. **It is necessary to see whether your house layout has been designed and built to take advantage of lucky number combinations.**

To decide whether or not you should change the period of your house requires a detailed analysis. Having said this, please note that all Period of 7 houses will lose energy as soon as we enter into Period 8. Many feng shui masters who understand Flying Star will insist that everyone should endeavour to change the period of their homes because of this reason alone.

This is because they know that the lowering of Chi strength afflicts houses of the immediately preceding period the most. This is a cardinal principle of Flying Star feng shui. This school of thought insists we MUST

revitalise the energy of our homes at the start of every change of period. If you are unable to do so, for instance because you live in an apartment, or if you do not have the finances to undertake the change, there are two choices facing you. First, consider looking for a new place, and second, you can take the risk and simply throw a big party to create massive yang energy, and hope that this will be sufficient to bring in the new energy of the new period.

In any case, you should look closely at how period 7 and 8 charts affect important rooms of your house, and how they affect the main door and facing palace. This will enable you to track the fortunes of different members of the family as you enter period 8. You can take your time to decide whether to change or not, but do develop awareness of how the new energy distribution is affecting the various occupants of your household.

CHI ENERGY of the Main Door

The Chi energy that surrounds the main door is of great importance in feng shui and it is not any different whether we practise Landscape Form School feng shui or Compass School feng shui. In Flying Star feng shui, the place where the main door is usually located is referred to as the Facing Palace, and it is vital to examine the quality and attributes of the energy in this part of the house. The facing palace is always at the front part of the house. Usually there will be either a main road or a large empty space or a view in front and the main door (or at least a large picture window) is placed here. However, do note that not all houses have the main door placed in the facing palace.

This is because it may NOT always be possible to do so. Also, from a feng shui perspective, it may not be the most auspicious location for the main door to be located there. First look for the main door on the layout plan. Next, look at the space defined by the facing palace. Note that for any house, the facing palace is always the center part of the front **one third** of the house.

You can determine the numbers that define the Chi there in Period 7 and also in Period 8. This is done by referring to the respective period 7 and 8 charts and looking at the numbers that apply to the facing palace.

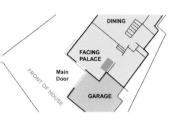

Compare the luck of the facing palace under the two charts. Look at the set of three numbers - the period number, the water star number and the mountain star number – that has flown into the facing palace in period 7 and then again in period 8.

These numbers are extracted from the flying star charts, which are in turn determined by the facing direction of your house. So now you realise that it is the **facing direction** of your house that determines its luck distribution. The charts summarising the luck of every room in all sixteen houses of each period are based on this

facing direction. So for your analysis to be accurate, you must identify and take this facing direction correctly.

To decide on whether to change the period of your house, compare the period 7 and period 8 numbers for the facing palace. If your facing palace has better numbers in the Period 8 chart, this single factor alone may be sufficient to warrant a change of period for your house. This is especially so if the main door is located in the facing palace, since the movement caused by the door being here (residents going in and out of the house) will strongly activate the good numbers.

How to Determine Facing Directions

Many people are confused by the term **facing direction**. Theoretically, the term facing direction can be defined, but at a practical level, you still have to use your judgement to decide. In the interests of accuracy, site investigation is almost always advisable. Also remember that the facing direction of the house or building is not always the same as the facing direction of its main door entrance. And different rules apply to apartments inside high-rise buildings!

FACING DIRECTION

Since this is such a crucial aspect of getting the flying star analysis correct, please note that you must look at your house carefully before deciding which direction you should take as your facing direction. Always use a reliable and proper compass. Estimating directions based on the angle of the sun is inefficient and inaccurate.

The facing direction of the house for purposes of determining the flying star chart is defined as the direction that:

- is facing the **source of maximum yang energy** and this can be a road, a market place, a cinema or a shopping complex.
- is facing a panoramic view, such as a view of valleys and distant mountains or a view of the city below or the view from a high-rise building.

The challenge is to determine the facing direction when it is uncertain, i.e. when there are two or more directions which seem to apply equally. In such cases, it may be necessary to analyse two or more charts and see which offers the best explanation of the luck of the house based on past experience of the residents.

Determining the facing direction of a house can sometimes be quite a challenge

Unobstructed view here

So is this the facing direction?

Main door is here

To accurately determine the facing direction of a building, one often requires an on-site investigation.

When In Doubt ...

There are many different situations when the **facing direction** is really difficult to determine, and without the correct facing direction, it is not possible to obtain an accurate reading of the luck of the residents within. When in doubt, the best way to determine the correct flying star chart to use is to study the charts of **both** directions that apply, and then see which one best describes the actual experiences of the residents within.

Note also that usually, the correct facing direction almost always has an opening into the home. The old texts always speak of the **eyes** and **mouth** of a home and it is believed that the doors and windows of the house symbolise the mouth and eyes of the house. We can say that it is the **face** of the house that determines its facing direction. This makes sense, since the door and windows allow incoming Chi to enter the house. So, in most instances, the main door is a good indication of the facing direction of the house. Now look at the illustration here and see if you are comfortable with the main door direction being the facing direction of the house shown here.

OBSERVE that the main door faces the road so it would appear reasonable to say that the facing direction of this house is **East**! Yet the large windows of the house facing the pond together with the pitch of the roofline would also suggest that the house facing direction is in actual fact **South**. Feng shui masters

will not all agree on which direction is the correct one. In my experience, I have discovered that in situations such as the one described here, it benefits to undertake two separate analyses using both directions, in this case, **East** and **South** as the facing direction. When the analyses are matched against the actual experiences of the residents, it will be easy to tell immediately which direction is the facing direction acknowledged by the invisible Chi of the environment.

Determine the facing direction

Check Several Times

Getting the **correct** facing direction of your home is crucial to your practice of Flying Star feng shui. I know of a practitioner in New York who studied with me and whose understanding of the method of Flying Star was excellent, but who tended to be rather lazy in the way he practised.

A las, almost always, he got the facing direction wrong, as a result of which his activation of the good luck sectors were also miserably wrong. He could not understand why his feng shui recommendations did not show results. A classmate of his, a lady from Down Under, who was a lot slower in understanding, but who made up for this by being extremely meticulous and careful, became a great deal more successful and has since become a BIG name in her area of practice. Her secret, she later confided in me, was that she almost always studied

more than one chart to ensure she did not make a mistake on the facing direction.

If you examine the houses shown here, you will see that even in simple cases such as the houses shown here, determining the facing direction can be a challenge. In these examples, you can see that the road and the field would suggest that the facing direction of the houses is the direction facing the road in front – very clear cut. But wait - note the view of the lake and the view of the golf course at the back of these houses. So the facing direction can be behind the houses.

Once again, it is usually not possible to determine with certainty what the facing direction is without a full on-site investigation. It is only then that you are able to see the terrain and feel the air. Often, the facing direction becomes crystal clear as soon as you see the site. It is then that your feng shui analysis will be more accurate.

Link houses here have back
    view of golf course

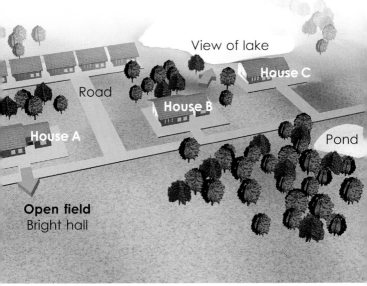

View of lake

House C

Road

House B

House A

Pond

Open field
Bright hall

What About Apartments?

Feng shui experts are not always in agreement on how the facing direction of high-rise apartments and high-rise condominiums are determined. This is because living in apartments that are very high up in the sky is akin to living in the high mountains, so that the Chi energy up there must surely be different from the Chi energy at ground level.

As a general rule, the flying star chart that applies to apartments should be based on the facing direction of the whole building. This makes good sense when we realise that the flying star chart applies to the whole building and your luck really depends on which corner of the building your apartment is located. I have found this to be absolutely accurate if the apartment is lower than the ninth floor. Apartments that are located above the ninth level have a different Chi distribution.

Up there in the sky, the Chi is different and the facing direction depends now on where there is a large balcony looking out to either a view of the city or a view of scenery – hills, lakes and so forth. Wherever there is a large balcony, it becomes obvious that the apartment is facing that direction – in which case the Flying Star chart that applies to the apartment will be based on that facing direction.

The illustration here shows a typical floor in an apartment building. Note there are three apartments on each floor, A, B and C, and each of these apartments face different directions. The apartments are also of different size.

Facing Direction of Apartments

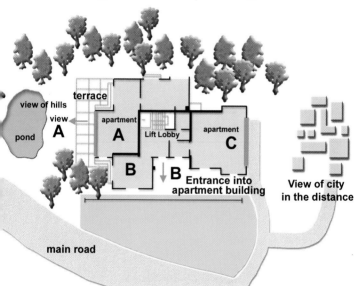

Apartment A

has a large balcony window, which faces a view of distant hills. It has a large terrace, which is accessed by large sliding glass doors. If you live in this apartment and you are located above the ninth floor, the flying star chart that determines your Chi distribution will very likely be based on the direction where there is a view of the hills in the distance. Thus, irrespective of the facing direction of the whole building, your flying star chart will differ from the chart determined by the building's facing direction.

Apartment B

is a small studio-sized apartment and its facing direction appears to be the same as the facing direction of the whole building. Here, irrespective of the floor location, the facing direction would be the same as for the whole building.

Apartment C

also has a large picture window that has a spectacular view of the city. This apartment does not have an outside terrace, but with the large picture window serving as the "mouth" of the apartment, this facing direction can be the basis for working out the flying star chart.

The picture on the right shows several beautiful high-rise buildings in a downtown city center. Note how **Villa Regency** serves as the back support for the building in the foreground, which enjoys the bright hall effect created by the field. This building also has a penthouse mansion in the sky .

Here the facing direction of the building and of its penthouse would be the same, i.e. facing the field.

APARTMENTS & CONDOMINIUMS

It is much harder to change the flying star period of apartments. This is because it is the whole building that will need new energy. To do this, it would be necessary to change the roof of the building, or at the very least give the apartment building a **face-lift** such as new coat of paint to symbolise a change of Chi energy.

Those living in apartments will need to coordinate with the managers of the building or with their neighbours. The collective benefits of revitalising the energy to move into the new period are sure to be worth the trouble of getting this organised.

How About Commercial Buildings?

The same rules apply to buildings irrespective of whether they are residential or commercial buildings. When applying Flying Star analysis to these high-rise buildings, it is very important to make careful assessment of the surroundings to ensure that the correct facing direction is used to select the charts for analysis. Most times you will note that the facing direction is the direction in which the building directly faces the road in front of it. However, there is uncertainty when the building is located at a junction, or at the end of a small *cul de sac*, or when it is on an elevated hill and the back of the building is overlooking a view. You also need to take into account elevated roads/highways.

The illustration on the right shows five buildings, which have been strategically positioned to highlight the different examples of facing directions.

Building A is sitting on slightly elevated land and while there is a road directly in front of it, the building actually faces the opposite direction and has a view of the city, which is a source of yang energy.

Building B is U-shaped, but it faces a small field which serves as its bright hall. Note that in this case, some may contend that the facing direction is at the front facing the oncoming road.

Building **C** has an entrance as shown by the red arrow, which is its correct facing direction. The road in front is elevated, so it is backing the building.

Building **D** faces a field, which is its bright hall.

Building **E** faces a valley.

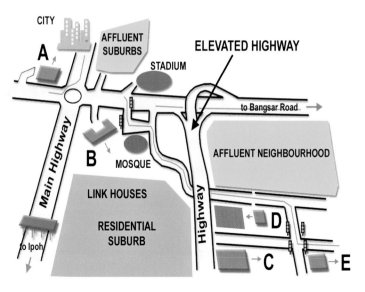

Always Use A Compass

When you have determined the facing direction that applies to your home/apartment/building, the next step is to invest in a good compass and then learn how to take and read directions accurately. Professional feng shui practitioners will use a special Luo Pan - the traditional feng shui compass - to take directions. For amateur practitioners, any modern well-made compass should be good enough.

A traditional feng shui Luo Pan is a complicated and scientific tool, which contains many secret formulas of the old schools of feng shui. Since many of these secrets require the use of the compass, and since there are many different meanings for every degree of compass direction, old style feng shui masters find the Luo Pan extremely useful.

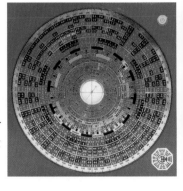

They can read the different meanings on every ring around the compass. Shown here is a condensed hand made Luo Pan designed and used by me in my classes on feng shui. The compass needle is placed in the center and simply by reading the direction from the compass, one is able to instantly take note of

the different meanings of the directions indicated. My Luo Pan incorporates the flying star charts for both periods 7 and 8, thus making it an extraordinarily useful tool.

For the amateur practitioner, however, it is not necessary to use such a sophisticated tool. A common western style compass, like the one shown here, is good enough. Just make certain it is an accurate compass. Use this to take the facing direction of your house and then select the flying star charts (of both periods) that are relevant to your analysis. I do want to stress that feng shui is a practice that relies very much on accurate compass readings, so it is necessary to own a compass if you really want to use this living skill to improve your luck. You should not use the sun to estimate your direction since this will not be accurate enough. Also, while the names of the directions (South, North, etc) may be placed on top or at the bottom of charts that you see in books, in practice, you must use the compass to determine the directions in your actual space.

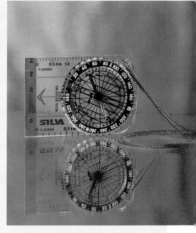

Houses That Face South

SOUTH facing houses belong to the East group of directions. The South-facing axis is thus an excellent facing direction for people belonging to the East group based on the Eight Mansions KUA formula of personalized feng shui.

In Flying Star feng shui, all the eight major directions are subdivided into 3 subdirections and these are referred to as the 24 mountains.

You must determine if your house facing direction is South 1, South 2 or South 3. These three subdirections are highlighted in the compass shown on the left here. Flying star charts are thus categorized according to the 24 mountain facing directions.

Subdirections S2 and S3 have the same chart.

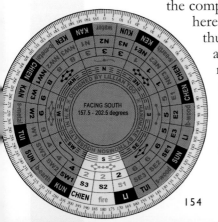

FACING SOUTH
157.5 - 202.5 degrees

154

PERIOD 7 and 8 CHARTS

The meanings of the charts for Period 7 houses facing South and for Period 8 houses facing South have been summarised in previous chapters. In this chapter, we will use examples of how the Period 7 and 8 charts can be compared in different types of houses and apartments.

Note: how the **water** and **mountain** stars of S1 charts always flip to the opposite direction when the facing direction is moved to S 2/3 and vice versa. This is a phenomenon which allows us to "move" the water and mountain star numbers from front to back and vice versa by simply shifting the facing direction a few degrees i..e. from S1 to S2/3 or vice versa. Look at the Period 8 charts shown below.

S 1 chart

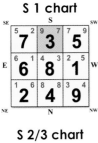

S 2/3 chart

Look at both charts. See how the double 8 mountain and water stars are in the North in a S1 chart and see how it flips to the South in a S2/3 chart.

Next, look at all the mountain and water stars in the other sectors.

You will observe the same phenomenon in respect of every sector. So just a few degrees of difference in your house facing direction can be enough to move the auspicious and inauspicious stars to their opposite directions, i.e. from front to back and from left to right.

South 2/3 Houses In Both Periods

PERIOD 7

Note that for this South 2/3 facing house, the Period 7 numbers show that the water star 8 is wasted in the garage. This wealth-bringing star number cannot do much for the family as it is "locked up" inside the garage. However, the mountain star 8 in the living room brings good health and harmonious relationship luck and when activated would bring good fortunes brought by "people luck". The master bedroom enjoys the 4 mountain star and the 1 water star. Thus, the numbers in the master bedroom would have brought good fortune to the couple living here. Most importantly, this chart is a **sum-of-ten** chart, which activates the period with the mountain star. So the period 7 chart has brought some excellent relationship luck for this household.

The main problem is the double 7 in the dining area. In Period 8, the double 7 will bring some traumatic misfortunes involving bloodshed and violence unless it is controlled, and this means using water and fire energy here. If this house is not changed to Period 8, the dining room should be painted red or blue to destroy/exhaust the double 7 stars here.

Analysis of Period 7 numbers in a S 2/3 house

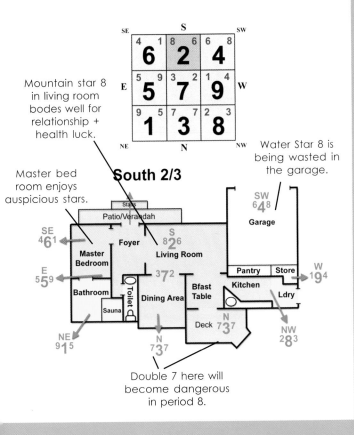

Mountain star 8 in living room bodes well for relationship + health luck.

Water Star 8 is being wasted in the garage.

Master bed room enjoys auspicious stars.

Double 7 here will become dangerous in period 8.

South 2/3 Houses In Both Periods

PERIOD 8

If the period of this house is changed in 2004 to that of Period 8, the facing palace of the house benefits enormously from the double 8 mountain and water stars. This combination benefits the entrance as well as the living room area of the house. This is a very auspicious indication, as the double 8 benefits in terms of money and relationship luck.

The master bedroom, however, is afflicted by the fighting star 3, which appears as the mountain star. This could cause disharmony between the couple unless it is suppressed with fire energy (something red). All other unlucky numbers of period 8 are either locked up in bathrooms or suppressed in the kitchen.

This house would, on balance, benefit from being changed to a period 8 house.

> **NOTE**: If this house were facing **South 1**, the auspicious double 8 water and mountain stars would be at the back of the house and would thus have been in the dining room area, and the master bedroom would have become seriously afflicted by the 5/9/2 combination. But if it stays a Period 7 house, it would suffer enormously from the double 7 turning evil as soon as Period 8 comes along. My recommendation for this house therefore would be to change to Period 8 and make sure the house faces South 2 or South 3.

Analysis of Period 8 numbers in the same S 2/3 house

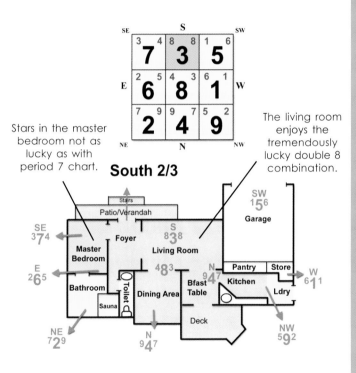

Stars in the master bedroom not as lucky as with period 7 chart.

The living room enjoys the tremendously lucky double 8 combination.

South 2/3

Houses That Face North

NORTH facing houses also belong to the East group of directions. A house facing North is said to be sitting South, so it also benefits from the north/south axis.

In Flying Star feng shui, all the eight major directions are subdivided into 3 subdirections and these are referred to as the 24 mountains.

Thus you must determine if your house facing direction is North 1, North 2 or North 3. These three subdirections are highlighted in the compass shown on the right here. Flying star charts are thus categorised according to the 24 mountain facing directions.

Subdirections N2 and N3 have the same chart.

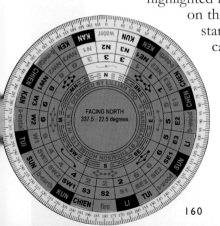

PERIOD 7 and 8 CHARTS

The meanings of both Period 7 and 8 charts have been summarised in previous chapters. In this chapter, we see how the charts are used to analyse the luck of houses.

Note: how the **water** and **mountain** stars of N1 charts always flip to the opposite direction when the facing direction is moved to N 2/3 and vice versa. This is a phenomenon which allows us to "move" the water and mountain star numbers either to the back and front of the house simply by shifting the facing direction of the house a few degrees i.e. from N1 to N2/3 or vice versa. Look at the Period 8 charts for North facing houses shown here.

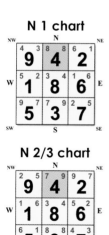

Look at the two period 8 charts shown here. See how the double 8 mountain and water stars are in the NORTH in a N1 chart and see how it flips to the South in a N2/3 chart.

The numbers are also very similar to those of a South-facing house.

Next look at all the mountain and water stars in the other sectors. You will observe the same phenomenon in respect of every sector. So just a few degrees of difference in your house facing direction can be enough to move the auspicious or inauspicious stars to their opposite directions, i.e. from front to back and from left to right. This is a very basic principle, which has very practical uses.

North 1 Houses In Both Periods

PERIOD 7

Note that for this North 1 facing house, the Period 7 numbers show that the water star 8 is strategically placed in the facing palace. This wealth-bringing star number is thus very well placed to bring "wealth" to the household if it is properly activated with a lively water feature. At the same time, the mountain star 8 is in the master bedroom and this brings good health and harmonious relationship luck to the couple living here. When activated, the mountain star 8 brings amazing "people luck".

Another good point is that the master bedroom enjoys the stunning 8/1/6 combination of white numbers, which brings excellent good fortune. This is a very good example of a house whose room layout is in sync with the flying star chart. Thus, residents of this house benefit strongly from being able to "tap" the good numbers. The auspicious double 7 is at the back of the house and also in bedroom 3. As the double 7 turns ugly in the next period, these areas will be afflicted then. Bedroom 2 is afflicted with the unlucky and disastrous combination of 3/2, which brings illness, legal entanglements, and all round bad luck.

Analysis of Period 7 numbers in a N 1 house

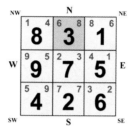

1　4 **8**	6　8 **3**	8　6 **1**
9　5 **9**	2　3 **7**	4　1 **5**
5　9 **4**	7　7 **2**	3　2 **6**

NW — N — NE
W — E
SW — S — SE

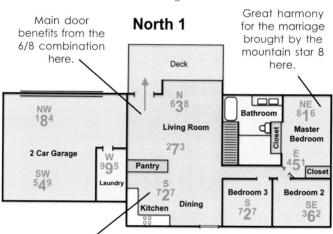

North 1

Main door benefits from the 6/8 combination here.

Great harmony for the marriage brought by the mountain star 8 here.

Deck

NW
1**8**4

2 Car Garage

SW
5**4**9

W
9**9**5

Pantry

Laundry

N
6**3**8

Living Room

2**7**3

S
7**2**7

Kitchen

Dining

Bathroom

Closet

Master Bedroom

NE
8**1**6

E
4**5**1

Closet

Bedroom 3

S
7**2**7

Bedroom 2

SE
3**6**2

This area will be afflicted next period when the double 7 s revert to their malevolent nature.

North 1 Houses In Both Periods

PERIOD 8

If the period of this house is changed in 2004 to that of Period 8, the facing palace of the house benefits immediately from the double 8 mountain and water stars. This combination benefits the entrance as well as the living room area of the house. This is a very auspicious indication as the double 8 benefits in terms of money and relationship luck. The star numbers in the master bedroom, however, are not as good, but they are also not bad. The fighting water star 3 appears locked up in the garage where it can do little harm.

The two bedrooms at the back of the house also do not benefit much from the change of energy to period 8. However, because the 7 loses energy at the change of period, it appears beneficial for this house to change its house period. It must, however, endeavour to maintain the North 1 facing direction as this benefits from the double 8 phenomenon.

NOTE: If this house were facing **North 2/3**, the auspicious double 8 water and mountain stars would be at the back of the house and would thus have been in the dining room area, and the master bedroom would have become seriously afflicted by the disastrous 9/5/7 combination. But if it stays a Period 7 house, it would suffer enormously from the double 7 turning evil. My recommendation for this house therefore would be to change to Period 8.

Analysis of Period 8 numbers in the same N 1 house

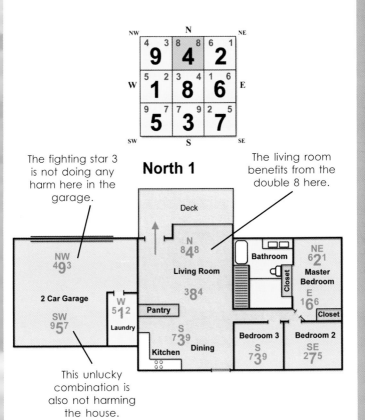

The fighting star 3 is not doing any harm here in the garage.

The living room benefits from the double 8 here.

North 1

This unlucky combination is also not harming the house.

Houses That Face Southwest

SOUTHWEST facing houses belong to the West group of directions. A house facing Southwest is said to be sitting Northeast, so it benefits from the very auspicious luck which all SW/NE axis houses enjoy during the Period 8.

In Flying Star feng shui, all eight major directions are subdivided into 3 subdirections and these are referred to as the 24 mountains.

You must determine if your house facing direction is Southwest 1, SW2 or SW3. These three subdirections are highlighted in the compass shown on the right here. flying star charts are thus categorised according to the 24 mountain facing directions.

Subdirections SW2 and SW3 have the same chart.

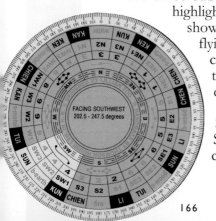

FACING SOUTHWEST
202.5 - 247.5 degrees

PERIOD 7 and 8 CHARTS

The meanings of both Period 7 and Period 8 charts have been summarised in previous chapters. In this chapter, we see how the charts are used to analyse the luck of houses.

In Period 8, all houses that are facing Southwest benefit from enormously auspicious flying star charts.

Note: that the auspicious water and mountain stars are very strategically placed in both charts i.e. in the facing and/or the sitting palace. In a SW1 house, the water star is placed in the facing palace, while in a SW2/3 chart, the mountain star 8 is placed in the facing palace.

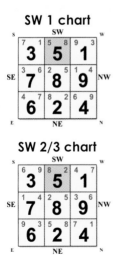

Look at the two Southwest charts shown here. Take note that a SW1 facing house enjoys the auspicious **sum of ten** combination chart while a SW2 facing house enjoys the equally auspicious **period string** combination chart. These are referred to as the SPECIALS in Flying Star feng shui jargon, said to attract enormous luck to households that have them — wealth, money, power, fame, popularity and big success. Those of you who may be thinking of building a new home in the Period of 8 would be well advised to try and design a house that can tap the SW/NE axis. This means having a **facing** or **sitting** direction of Southwest. Sitting SW requires the house to face NE.

Southwest 1 Houses In Both Periods

PERIOD 7

During Period 7, this house benefited enormously from the strategically placed double 7 mountain and water star in the facing palace. Many SW houses also benefited in a similar manner. However when the period changes to Period 8, the number 7 reverts to its old evil nature and instead of bringing good fortune, the double 7 will now bring violence, bloodshed and also signify the danger that household members could be the victims of armed robbery.

For SW facing houses, therefore, there is no doubt at all that they should change the period of their house. This will enable them to escape the ill effects of the 7 transforming to evil and enable them to tap into the MEGA auspicious numbers of the Period 8 Southwest-facing charts. Meanwhile, note in the example shown here how the center numbers of the Period 7 chart is the auspicious **parent string** combination of 1/7/4 and in this house, note how the open-plan layout enables this number at the center of the house to flow to other parts of the house. This is an excellent way of benefitting from good numbers.

Analysis of Period 7 numbers in a SW 1 house

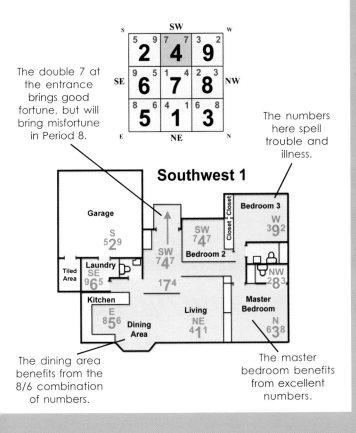

The double 7 at the entrance brings good fortune, but will bring misfortune in Period 8.

The numbers here spell trouble and illness.

Southwest 1

The dining area benefits from the 8/6 combination of numbers.

The master bedroom benefits from excellent numbers.

Southwest 1 Houses In Both Periods

PERIOD 8

This is a perfect example of a house whose facing direction dictates that it simply must change to Period 8 to reap fantastic abundance and success luck. Look closely at the numbers in the Period 8 chart superimposed onto the house here. First note the **sum-of-ten** combination, which brings excellent relationship and health luck. This spells harmony and success in the household, and for those who appreciate the joys of a happy family life, this chart will bring you what you want. In a SW 1 facing house, you can see that the water star 8 is in the facing palace. Thus, placing water in front of the house would bring enormous wealth luck. This is because the **indirect spirit** of Period 8 is also in the Southwest, and when water is placed in the location of the indirect spirit, it is said to attract plenty of money luck.

NOTE: If this house were facing **Southwest 2/3**, it would enjoy the **parent string** combination and the facing palace would benefit from the mountain star 8. In such a house however, the water feature must not be placed in front, as this would cause the auspicious mountain star 8 to "fall into the water". For those wanting to create massive wealth luck, change to Period 8 and make sure your facing direction is in the first sub sector, i.e. facing the SW1 direction.

Analysis of Period 8 numbers in the same SW 1 house

This house now benefits from the sum-of-ten combination.

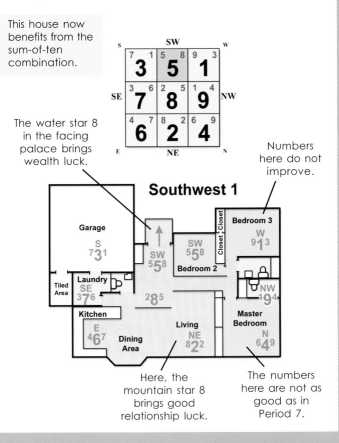

The water star 8 in the facing palace brings wealth luck.

Numbers here do not improve.

Here, the mountain star 8 brings good relationship luck.

The numbers here are not as good as in Period 7.

Houses That Face Northeast

NORTHEAST facing houses belong to the West group of directions. A house facing is Northeast benefits from the very auspicious luck which all SW/NE axis houses enjoy during the Period 8. This facing direction also corresponds to the number 8 – thus, it should not come as a surprise that the NE facing charts enjoy the same SPECIALS that make the SW facing house so auspicious in Period 8.

Flying star charts are categorised according to the 24 mountain facing directions.

You must therefore determine if your house facing direction is Northeast 1, NE 2 or NE3.

These three subdirections are highlighted in the compass shown on the left here. Subdirections NE2 and NE3 have the same flying star chart.

FACING NORTHEAST
22.5 - 67.5 degrees

PERIOD 7 and 8 CHARTS

The meanings of the Period 7 and 8 charts have already been summarised in previous chapters.

In Period 8, all houses that are facing Northeast will benefit from enormously auspicious flying star charts.

Note: that the auspicious water and mountain stars are very strategically placed in both charts i.e. in the facing and/or the sitting palace. In a NE1 house, the water star is placed in the facing palace, while in a NE2/3 chart, the mountain star 8 is placed in the facing palace. It is thus important to place water and mountain features correctly in accordance with the chart that applies.

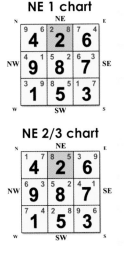

Look at the two NE charts shown here. Take note that a NE1 facing house enjoys the auspicious **sum-of-ten** combination chart while a NE 2/3 facing house enjoys the equally auspicious **period string** combination chart. Just like the SW facing houses. These are referred to as the SPECIALS in Flying Star feng shui jargon, said to attract enormous luck to households that have them — wealth, money, power, fame, popularity and big success. Those of you who may be thinking of building a new home in the Period of 8 would be well advised to try and design a house that can tap the SW/NE axis. This means having a **facing** or **sitting** direction of Northeast. Sitting NE requires the house to face SW.

Northeast 2/3 Houses in both Periods

PERIOD 7

During Period 7, this NE 2/3 house benefited enormously from the strategically placed double 7 mountain and water star in the facing palace. Many NE houses also benefited from this same double 7 formation. However, when the period changes to Period 8, the number 7 reverts to its original dangerous character and instead of bringing good fortune, the double 7 will now bring violence, bloodshed and also signify that household members could be the victims of armed robbery.

For NE-facing houses, therefore, there is no doubt at all that they should change the period of their house. This will enable them to escape from the ill effects of the 7, as well as enable them to tap into the MEGA auspicious numbers of the Period 8 Northeast-facing charts. Note in the example shown here how the center numbers of the Period 7 chart is the auspicious **parent string** combination of 4/7/1 and in this house, note how the dining room being here benefits from this. Note the master bedroom afflicted by the dangerous 9/5 combination. Also note the auspicious mountain and water stars 8 are behind the house and are thus wasted.

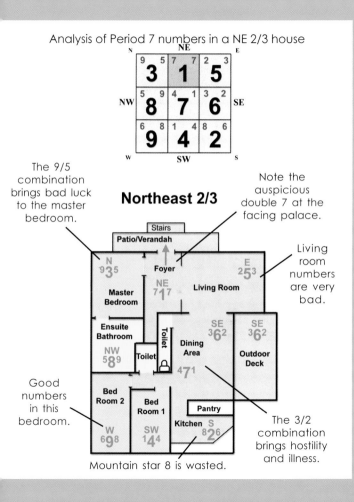

Analysis of Period 7 numbers in a NE 2/3 house

	NE	
9 5 **3**	7 7 **1**	2 3 **5**
5 9 **8**	4 1 **7**	3 2 **6**
6 8 **9**	1 4 **4**	8 6 **2**

N   E   NW   SE   W   SW   S

Northeast 2/3

The 9/5 combination brings bad luck to the master bedroom.

Note the auspicious double 7 at the facing palace.

Living room numbers are very bad.

Stairs

Patio/Verandah

Foyer

N ⁹**3**⁵

Master Bedroom

NE ⁷**1**⁷

Living Room

E ₂**5**³

Ensuite Bathroom

Toilet

SE ₃**6**²

NW ₅**8**⁹

Toilet

Dining Area

SE ₃**6**²

Outdoor Deck

₄**7**¹

Good numbers in this bedroom.

Bed Room 2

Bed Room 1

Pantry

The 3/2 combination brings hostility and illness.

W ₆**9**⁸

SW ₁**4**⁴

Kitchen

S ₈**2**⁶

Mountain star 8 is wasted.

Northeast 2/3 Houses in both Periods

PERIOD 8

This is a another example of a house whose facing direction dictates that it absolutely must change to Period 8 to reap serious wealth and health luck for the next twenty years. Look closely at the numbers in the Period 8 chart superimposed onto the house here. First note the **sum-of-ten** combination brings excellent wealth and prosperity luck. This combination is that of the wealth bringing water star with the period star, and their presence in every sector of the chart spells career and business luck for the household. Those just starting out in life would benefit enormously from this chart if they can find or build a house that can successfully tap these numbers. In a NE2/3-facing house, you can see that the water star 8 is in the facing palace. Thus, placing water in front of the house would bring enormous wealth luck. Meanwhile, the mountain star 8 is at the back, so building a high wall behind would be excellent.

NOTE: If this house were facing **Northeast 1**, it would enjoy the **parent string** combination and the sitting palace would benefit from the water star 8. In such a house, placing a water feature behind would enable residents to tap the **Indirect spirit** of the house – a most auspicious occurrence. For those wanting to create massive wealth luck, change to Period 8. Both the NE facing charts are equally good.

Analysis of Period 8 numbers in the same NE 2/3 house

The house enjoys the auspicious sum-of-ten if it changes to Period 8.

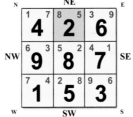

N	NE	E
1 7 **4**	8 5 **2**	3 9 **6**
NW 6 3 **9**	5 2 **8**	4 1 **7** SE
7 4 **1**	2 8 **5**	5 9 **3**
W	SW	S

Northeast 2/3

Mountain star 8 in the facing palace brings excellent relationship luck.

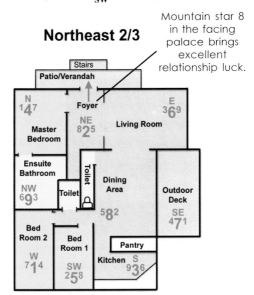

Houses That Face East

EAST facing houses are favourable for those whose KUA numbers are part of the East group based on Eight Mansions feng shui. However, in the Period of 7, all East facing houses had to endure the period **five yellow** being parked in its facing palace so that whenever bad luck visited the house due to the annual 5 such as happened in 2002, the bad luck would become very intense. It is thus a very good idea to liberate the facing palace from the five yellow by taking advantage of the change in period to change the house chi energy to that of period 8. This will move the deadly 5 out of the facing palace.

Flying star charts are categorised according to the 24 mountain facing directions. You must therefore determine if your house facing direction is East 1, East 2 or East 3.

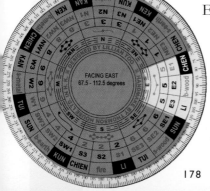

These three subdirections are highlighted in the compass shown on the left here. Subdirections E2 and E3 have the same flying star chart.

PERIOD 7 and 8 CHARTS

The meanings of the Period 7 and 8 charts have already been summarised in previous chapters.

In Period 8, all houses facing East benefit from the auspicious double 8 mountain and water stars being either in the Facing palace or in the Sitting palace. This is shown in the East-facing Period 8 charts below.

Note: It appears more auspicious from a wealth luck dimension to opt for an East 1 facing direction, as this enables residents to capture the good effects of having the double 8 at the front of the house. This enables water to be activated at the front of the house to bring wealth.

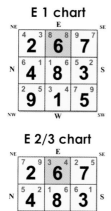

From the charts, note that in an East1 facing house, the double 8 is in the Facing palace. Since this is also the East direction, placing water here would be most auspicious, as this also activates the water star. The center numbers comprise the 1/8/6 combination of white stars, which are incredibly auspicious. An open concept for the center of the house would ensure that this auspicious combination is felt throughout the house.

If the house faces the second and third sub-directions of East, the double 8 flies to the Sitting palace - then it is more beneficial to activate the mountain star 8 by building a wall behind the house.

East 1 Houses in both Periods

PERIOD 7

During Period 7, this East 1 house had all its good luck numbers wasted in the garage and store room. The best that could be done was to "activate" the auspicious water star 8 as a small tai chi in the living room as shown. But for the most part, the water star 8 was "locked inside the garage". However the auspicious mountain star 8 flew into the master bedroom bringing excellent family luck for the couple.

For this house, it appears that while the Period of 7 did not bring money luck, it very likely brought other dimensions of good fortune such as good health, popularity and good relationships luck. It is a good idea for this house to revitalise its Chi energy, as most other sectors have weak number combinations.

The important consideration here is to see how the Period 8 numbers affect the master bedroom, the living room and the facing palace.

Analysis of Period 7 numbers in an E 1 house

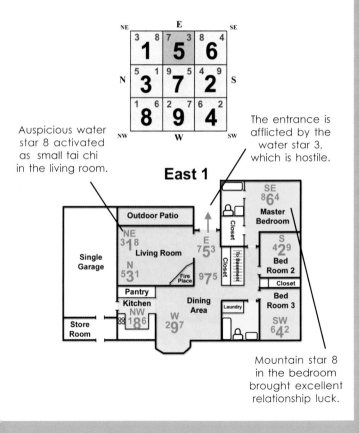

Auspicious water star 8 activated as small tai chi in the living room.

The entrance is afflicted by the water star 3, which is hostile.

East 1

Mountain star 8 in the bedroom brought excellent relationship luck.

East 1 Houses in both Periods

PERIOD 8

The good news is that in the Period of 8, East facing houses enjoy the double 8 combination, and in an East 1 house, the double 8 flies into the Facing palace. This indicates good fortune for this house, as the layout allows the good fortune to "flow into the living room as well as to the rest of the house in a seamless manner. With the water star 8 in front and since the front is East, water here is beneficial and brings great good fortune.

What is also good for the house is that the hostile water star 3 is in the NE and is thus locked up inside the garage. The center stars of 1/8/6 reside in the corridor, which is a conduit of Chi flow. Thus good luck can travel through the house efficiently and effectively. If the walls separating the living room and dining room were removed, it would be even more auspicious for the house, since this would focus even more strongly on the auspicious center numbers.

NOTE: If this house were facing **East 2/3**, the double 8 mountain and water stars would flip to the back of the house, benefiting the dining room. If the family uses the dining room regularly and eats at home most of the time, they will benefit from the double 8. The auspicious combination of 4 water and 6 period in the facing palace would bring plenty of secret admirers for the household residents. It is vital then not to place water in the front, as this could cause extramarital affairs.

Analysis of Period 8 numbers in the same E 1 house

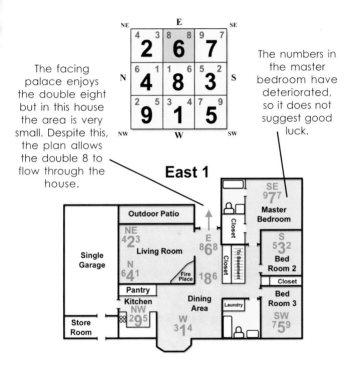

The facing palace enjoys the double eight but in this house the area is very small. Despite this, the plan allows the double 8 to flow through the house.

The numbers in the master bedroom have deteriorated, so it does not suggest good luck.

	NE	E	SE
	4 3 **2**	8 8 **6**	9 7 **7**
N	6 1 **4**	1 6 **8**	5 2 **3**	S
	2 5 **9**	3 4 **1**	7 9 **5**
	NW	W	SW

East 1

- Outdoor Patio
- NE 4²3 Living Room
- N 6⁴1
- Fire Place
- Single Garage
- Pantry
- Kitchen
- NW 2⁹5
- Store Room
- W 3¹4
- Dining Area
- Laundry
- E 8⁶8
- 18⁶
- Closet
- Closet
- To Basement
- SE 9⁷7 Master Bedroom
- S 5³2 Bed Room 2
- Closet
- Bed Room 3
- SW 7⁵9

Houses That Face West

WEST facing houses are favourable for those whose KUA numbers are part of the West group based on Eight Mansions feng shui. During Period 7, West facing houses did not benefit much from a lacklustre chart. Those familiar with feng shui will have realised that the facing palace numbers were not as good as the numbers on either side of it. The main door would thus have benefited if it had been moved wither to the left or right of the front of the house. This is because in W2/3 facing houses the water star 8 is in the Northwest and the mountain star 8 is in the Southwest in the front part of the house.

Flying star charts are categorised according to the 24 mountain facing directions. You must therefore determine if your house facing direction is West 1, West 2 or West 3.

These three subdirections are highlighted in the compass shown on the left here. Subdirections W2 and W3 have the same flying star chart.

PERIOD 7 and 8 CHARTS

The meanings of the Period 7 and 8 charts have already been summarised in previous chapters.

In Period 8, all houses facing West benefit from the auspicious double 8 mountain and water stars being either in the facing palace or in the sitting palace. This is shown in the West facing Period 8 charts below.

Note: It appears more auspicious from a wealth luck dimension to opt for a West 2/3 facing direction, as this enables residents to capture the good effects of having the double 8 at the front of the house. This enables water to be activated at the front of the house to bring wealth.

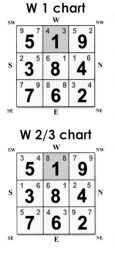

W 1 chart

W 2/3 chart

From the charts, note that in a West 1 facing house, the double 8 is in the sitting palace. Here, it is more beneficial to activate the mountain star 8 to provide support for the house. If the house faces the second and third sub-directions of West, the double 8 flies to the facing palace. It would benefit the household s wealth luck if a water feature is located here to activate the water star 8. Meanwhile, the center numbers comprise the 6/8/1 combination of white stars, which are incredibly auspicious. An open-space concept for the center of the house would ensure that this auspicious combination is felt throughout the house.

West 2/3 Houses in both Periods

PERIOD 7

During Period 7, this West 2/3 house is afflicted by the difficult numbers of 5 and 9 in the center and the 3 mountain star in the facing palace. This causes legal entanglements and twenty years of relationship problems. Meanwhile, the center numbers cause illness, loss and general bad luck and misfortunes. In this house, however, there are small rooms in the center (the store room and the toilet), which can be interpreted as "locking" up the inauspicious star numbers of the center so they do not cause great misfortune for the household.

For this house, the water star 8 has flown into the bedroom 3, making it difficult to activate wealth luck for the house. But it does bring good luck to residents residing in this room. The mountain star 8 is in the living room, and this can be activated.

To decide whether or not this house should change to Period 8, we should see if the numbers in the facing palace can be improved.

Analysis of Period 7 numbers in a W 2/3 house

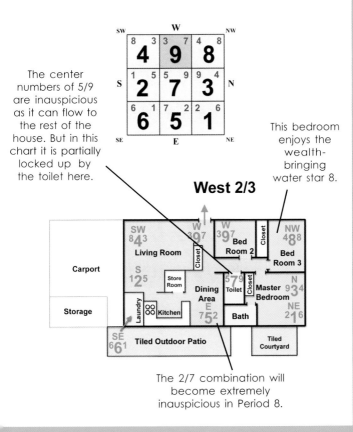

The center numbers of 5/9 are inauspicious as it can flow to the rest of the house. But in this chart it is partially locked up by the toilet here.

This bedroom enjoys the wealth-bringing water star 8.

West 2/3

The 2/7 combination will become extremely inauspicious in Period 8.

West 2/3 Houses in both Periods

PERIOD 8

The good news is that in the Period of 8, all West 2/3 facing houses enjoy the double 8 combination, which flies into its facing palace. This indicates very good fortune for the household if they know how to activate it. The center numbers are also auspicious as it is the combination of white numbers 6/8/1. Alas, these lucky numbers are "locked up" inside the toilet. Make sure this does not happen in your house.

The hostile 3 water star is in the dining room, while the master bedroom has to put up with two sets of unlucky numbers, the 2/5 and the 9/7. The master bedroom is thus badly afflicted.

NOTE: If this house were facing **West 1**, the double 8 mountain and water stars would flip to the back of the house benefiting the Dining room. If the family uses the dining room regularly, they will benefit from the double 8. Despite the lack of lucky sectors in Period 8, nevertheless, the incidence of the double 8 water and mountain stars being in the facing or sitting palace is sufficient reason to change the house to Period 8.

Analysis of Period 8 numbers in the same W 2/3 house

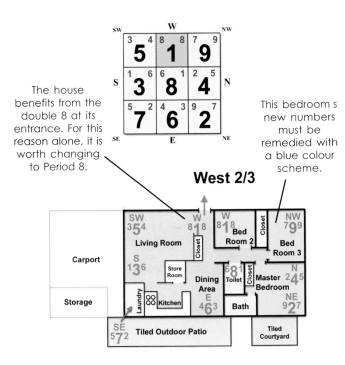

The house benefits from the double 8 at its entrance. For this reason alone, it is worth changing to Period 8.

This bedroom s new numbers must be remedied with a blue colour scheme.

Houses That Face Northwest

NORTHWEST facing houses are favourable for those whose KUA numbers are part of the West group based on Eight Mansions feng shui. During Period 7, all Northwest facing houses that had a view of a big building or some elevated land in front would have benefited from the auspicious mountain star in the facing palace. Houses facing the first sub-direction NW 1 had the auspicious 8 mountain star, while those in NW 2/3 would have benefited from the mountain star 7. This would have been made even more auspicious with a water feature in the center – such as an aquarium, as the water star 8 is in the center of the house. Flying star charts are categorised according to the 24 mountain facing directions. You must therefore determine if your house facing direction is NW 1, NW 2 or NW 3. These three subdirections are highlighted in the compass shown here. Sub-directions NW 2 and NW 3 have the same flying star chart.

FACING NORTHWEST
292.5 - 337.5 degrees

PERIOD 7 and 8 CHARTS

The meanings of the Period 7 and 8 charts have already been summarized in previous chapters. In Period 8, all houses facing Northwest benefit from very auspicious numbers in the facing and sitting palaces. This is shown in the NW Period 8 charts shown here. Note the auspicious 8 mountain and water stars and also take note of the other numbers accompanying them i.e. 1 and 6. Properly activated, a Period 8 NW house can bring enormous benefits to the patriarch of the household.

Note: It appears more auspicious from a wealth luck dimension to opt for an NW 2/3 facing direction as this enables residents to capture the good effects of having the water star 8 at the front of the house. Activating the front of the house with water will then bring wealth.

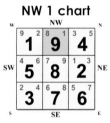

From the charts, note that in a NW 1 facing house, the auspicious 8 mountain star is in the facing palace, and this flies to the sitting palace at the back when the facing direction is NW 2/3.

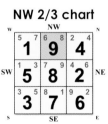

In the same way, look at the place of the auspicious water star 8. It flies to the facing palace in a NW 2/3 house and into the sitting palace at the back in a NW 1 facing house. The center numbers 7/8/9 are said to be consecutive numbers and this makes them a lucky combination.

Northwest 1 Houses in both Periods

PERIOD 7

During Period 7, this NW 1 house benefits from the mountain star 8 flying into the master bedroom. This brings excellent relationship and health luck to the patriarch and matriarch of the family. The water star 8 is in the center of the house, so a water feature here would be most beneficial.

Unfortunately, note the kitchen has been placed next to the facing palace and a pantry has been built in the center of the house. This effectively "locks up" the auspicious water star 8, and the effect of this is to cause the household to suffer from a perpetual shortage of money.

The living and dining room areas, however, do benefit from the auspicious 7 mountain star bringing harmony and goodwill to the household. This comes to an end when period 8 takes over.

Indeed, the 7 mountain star in the living room becomes a source of burglary Chi in the Period of 8. Thus, the house will benefit from a change of period.

Analysis of Period 7 numbers in a NW 1 house

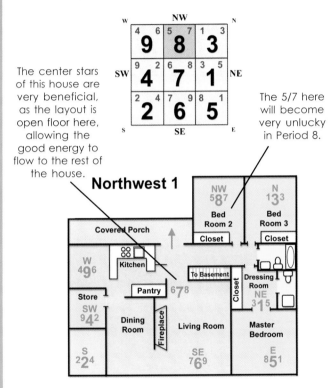

The center stars of this house are very beneficial, as the layout is open floor here, allowing the good energy to flow to the rest of the house.

The 5/7 here will become very unlucky in Period 8.

Northwest 1 Houses in both Periods

PERIOD 8

In Period 8, the NW 1 facing house has the mountain star 8 in its facing palace. This indicates good fortune for the household. Here, the covered porch should be made of tiles and concrete materials to activate the lucky mountain star 8. The center numbers are also auspicious, as they make up the combination of **continuous numbers** 7/8/9.

The living room area also benefits from the excellent 6/7/8 combination, which incorporates the auspicious water star 8. Placing an aquarium here in the Southeast part of the living area will activate wealth luck for the family.

NOTE: If this house were facing **Northwest 2/3,** the water star 8 would have flipped into the facing palace, in which case, a water feature in the front of the house would be most beneficial to the household. However, if this house had a NW 2/3 chart, the illness star 2 would have flown into the master bedroom, bringing illness and sickly energy, which would have been made worse by the 9 mountain star.

So, on balance, I would recommend that a NW 1 house for Period 8 would be a better chart for this particular house, but for others, a NW 2/3 chart having the water star 8 in the front can be very beneficial in terms of wealth accumulation. The secret is, of course, to know how to effectively activate the auspicious water star 8.

Analysis of Period 8 numbers in the same NW 1 house

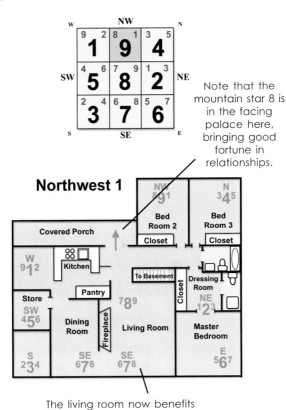

Note that the mountain star 8 is in the facing palace here, bringing good fortune in relationships.

The living room now benefits from the water star 8.

Houses That Face Southeast

SOUTHEAST facing houses are favourable for those whose KUA numbers are part of the East group based on Eight Mansions feng shui. During Period 7, Southeast facing houses have the auspicious water and mountain stars 7 in the facing and sitting palaces, as well as the lucky 8/7/6 combination in the center. The chart thus brings a very lucky "spine" to the house, benefiting houses that have depth. Flying star charts are categorised according to the 24 mountain facing directions. You must therefore determine if your house facing direction is SE 1, SE 2 or SE 3.

These three subdirections are highlighted in the compass shown on the left here. Subdirections SE 2 and SE 3 have the same flying star chart.

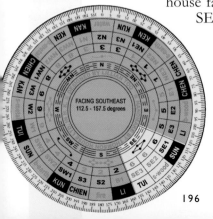

FACING SOUTHEAST
112.5 - 157.5 degrees

PERIOD 7 and 8 CHARTS

The meanings of the Period 7 and 8 charts have already been summarised in previous chapters. In Period 8, all houses facing Southeast benefits from the auspicious water and mountain stars 8 being either in the facing palace or in the sitting palace. This is shown in the SE Period 8 charts reproduced below.

Note: It appears more auspicious from a wealth luck dimension to opt for an SE 2/3 facing direction, as this enables residents to capture the good effects of having the water star 8 at the front of the house (which activates wealth luck) and the mountain star at the back (which can be activated for support and relationship luck).

SE 1 chart

SE 2/3 chart

Note that in a SE 1 facing house, the mountain star 8 is in the facing palace. In a SE 2/3 facing chart, the water star 8 is in the facing palace. Since the SE direction benefits from water, a SE 2/3 chart is more beneficial, since placing water here also activates the water star. The center numbers comprise the 7/8/9 combination of **continuous numbers**, which bring harmony and success. An open concept for the center would ensure this auspicious combination is felt throughout the house. The numbers of the other sectors are not especially good, but focusing on the central spine of the house will bring good fortune for the residents. This alone enforces any decision to change the period of the house.

Southeast 2/3 Houses in both Periods

PERIOD 7

During Period 7, the water star 5 in the facing palace afflicts this SE 2/3 house. This brings financial misfortunes and it would have been beneficial to move the front door to the left or right (i.e. to the South or East sectors). This is hard to do for this house, since the master bedroom is in the East and the kitchen is in the South. It is thus beneficial to enter the house from the garage at the back.

The good news for this house is that it does benefit from what is known as its **Pearl String** combination which is auspicious. This means that every sector has a set of continuous numbers, which brings overall success and harmony. This combination also has the power to overcome many of the afflictions brought by the 5 misfortune and the 2 illness star.

However, in order for the combination to become activated requires the house to have a regular shape, either square or rectangular. In the example here, this is not the case. But it can easily be made "regular" with lights strategically installed at the back.

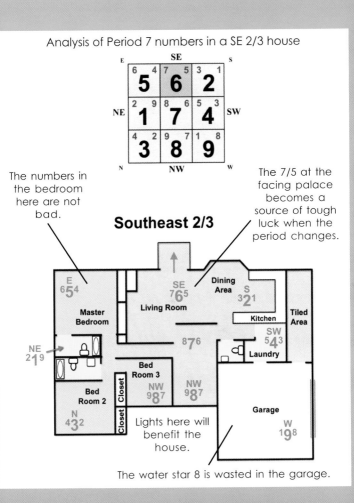

Analysis of Period 7 numbers in a SE 2/3 house

E	SE	S
6 · 4 · **5**	7 · 5 · **6**	3 · 1 · **2**
NE		SW
2 · 9 · **1**	8 · 6 · **7**	5 · 3 · **4**
	NW	
4 · 2 · **3**	9 · 7 · **8**	1 · 8 · **9**

The numbers in the bedroom here are not bad.

The 7/5 at the facing palace becomes a source of tough luck when the period changes.

Southeast 2/3

E 6**5**4

SE 7**6**5   Dining Area

Living Room

S 3**2**1

Master Bedroom

Kitchen

Tiled Area

NE 2**1**9

8**7**6

SW 5**4**3

Laundry

Bed Room 3

Bed Room 2

Closet   Closet

NW 9**8**7   NW 9**8**7

N 4**3**2

Garage

W 1**9**8

Lights here will benefit the house.

The water star 8 is wasted in the garage.

Southeast 2/3 Houses in both Periods

PERIOD 8

If this house changes to Period 8, it will benefit from having a very strong and lucky central "spine". This is because the water and mountain stars 8 fly into the facing and sitting palaces, which brings excellent money and health luck. And if properly activated with the correct placement of water and crystals, this would attract exceptional luck.

In addition, the central numbers 9/8/7 are also auspicious. For this particular house, which faces SE 2/3, the water star 8 is in the front, so changing to Period 8 is beneficial. Build a pond in front of the house to activate the auspicious water star for it to bring wealth and increased prosperity.

NOTE: If this house were facing **Southeast 1,** the 8 mountain star would flip to the front of the house, in which case building a pond in front would be fatal, since this would cause this auspicious mountain star to "fall into the water". Whenever an auspicious mountain star falls into a hole or into water, residents will suffer a great deal of employee problems. Relationships with everyone and amongst themselves will not be smooth and will seem to be perpetually hostile. So it is vital to get the facing direction correct when activating with water.

Analysis of Period 8 numbers in the same SE 2/3 house

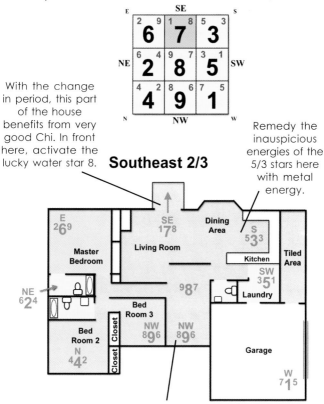

With the change in period, this part of the house benefits from very good Chi. In front here, activate the lucky water star 8.

Remedy the inauspicious energies of the 5/3 stars here with metal energy.

Southeast 2/3

The mountain star 8 behind benefits from a wall feature at the back.

Activating Auspicious Water Stars For Wealth

Chapter 5

Water Brings Wealth

One reason why Flying Star feng shui is so compelling is that it offers a very potent method for using water to activate wealth luck. The method requires activating the auspicious **water stars** of the house - outside in the garden, as well as inside the house, especially in the living areas that are most frequented by residents. Identifying exactly where these **lucky stars** are takes account of time formulas, because all luck sectors, including money luck sectors, change over time. Activating these sectors requires the building of water structures such as pools, ponds or waterfalls.

One long-standing Taoist feng shui master from Hong Kong once told me, "If you want to use feng shui to improve your finances, you must know how to find the **money spot** in your house or property. And then you must build a water feature there. A beautiful swimming pool is good." He was very insistent that water feng shui based on flying star charts was very potent for improving money luck. He explained there were different feng shui theories about wealth luck, but the one he had most faith in was the system of feng shui that activates the water stars or **siang sin** (the facing stars), which are the wealth stars of the flying star chart.

"When you build a suitable yang water feature where a

lucky water star is found, **money will start to flow in**. In both the Period 7 and period of 8, the wealth spot of any house or building is where the water star 8 is located.

Make sure water flows **towards** the house and never away from the house.

The Water Star

Once you understand how to choose the correct flying star chart that applies to your house, you will be able to locate the money luck sectors in and around your house. The water star symbolises the wealth or money luck of the building. When the water star number is lucky, it brings wonderful money luck not only to the sector it occupies, but also to the entire household when it is activated. And when it is an unlucky or afflicted number, it will likewise bring financial loss to the entire household if it gets inadvertently activated. This is why water should always be placed carefully, otherwise there is the danger that it might be in a sector where the water star is inauspicious. Or worse, it might be in a sector that **harms** other lucky stars.

If a good water star is in the South

If the water star 8 is in the South, note that placing water here would clash with the element of the South, which is Fire. This would seem to flout conventional feng shui wisdom, since the presence of water in the South is said to affect one's good name and douse out recognition luck under different systems of feng shui. So when the water star 8 flies to the South, it presents a real dilemma. For expert masters of feng shui, however, this is not a problem, since their knowledge of the five elements enable them to find effective solutions. According to them, when the flying water star 8 enters the South, it presents the opportunity for Water and Fire to combine effectively to produce **steam** – and this symbolizes power!

If a bad water star is in the North, East, or Southeast

These three directions always benefit from water because North is the direction of water, while East and Southeast are directions of the wood element that also benefit from water. Thus, conventional wisdom in feng shui suggests that placing water features in these sectors will always be beneficial to the household. This is why it is beneficial to place water in these sectors of your household, and especially in the Southeast, which symbolises wealth under the Pa Kua Eight Aspirations method of feng shui.

What happens then when an unlucky flying water star number such as 2, 3 or 5 occupies any of these directions? With water there, surely it will activate the unlucky water star, which then brings inauspicious luck to the household? This does not apply as much to 2 and 5, since these are earth numbers, but it does strengthen the quarrelsome 3, which is a wood number. Having said this, it would be better to fine-tune your practice of feng shui by **not** having water in these sectors when the water star here is an unlucky number, especially if the water feature is a large swimming pool, waterfall or fountain.

Just like the sun's heat causes water to evaporate and rise to form clouds that bring the rain, so too will the presence of water in the South attract the good fortune of power and wealth when the auspicious flying water star is in the South. This happens when the lucky 8 is the water star. This occurs to Period 7 houses that face North 2/3 and SW 2/3 and also to Period 8 houses that face South 2/3 and North 2/3. These houses have the opportunity to activate very powerful wealth luck. Here, understanding the deeper interpretation of the five elements will enable them to activate water in the South with confidence when the auspicious flying water star flies to the South.

The Number Eight

Under the Flying Star system, the number 8 is already the most auspicious number, since it is the strongest of the white numbers. It is also the strongest of the Earth numbers. During the Period of 8, the luck of this number is multiplied further. The number 8 is the number that rules the period between 2004 and 2024, so that during this twenty-year period, the number 8 becomes incredibly special. In Period 7, and more so in Period 8, the sector that houses the water star 8 in your house or building is the luckiest sector to place water.

So why is the number 8 so lucky?

Firstly, 8 is one of the trinity of white numbers (the other white numbers are 1 and 6) which are

also considered to be lucky numbers. Indeed, of the three numbers, the 8 is the strongest during this **Lower Period** of the whole 180 year cycle.

Secondly, 8 is also one of the three earth numbers. The other two numbers are 5 and 2. When combined with these two other earth numbers, the combination is said to be a **Parent String** combination, and is very auspicious indeed. Here, 8 stands for mountain, which suggests a time of preparation. The mountain is filled with treasures of the earth. The direction of 8 is Northeast, which is an Earth sector. Since feng shui has to do with Earth luck, 8 becomes incredibly vital.

Thirdly, in the period of 8, precisely because it is its period, the number takes on fresh new energy, what is referred to in feng shui terminology as young yang energy. This means that 8 has the power to expand and grow as well. As the period number, it is said to possess tremendous vitality and strength. No other number will have the same level of yang Chi potency as the number 8 during the twenty years from 2004 to 2024. Thus, when 8 appears either as a water star number, as a mountain star number or as an annual or month number in any sector, it brings fresh new vitality and good fortune to that sector at the time when it occupies the sector.

Meanwhile, note that 8 is also the infinity sign, which is one of the powerful mystical signs believed to possess extraordinary vitality in many traditions pictured here is our stunning crystal and gold infinity 8 symbol given to us by a dear friend for good luck (facing page).

Activating Your Water Star 8

One of the most important ways of activating money luck in any house or building is to energise the sector occupied by the **flying water star 8**. Locating it depends on the period of your house, because the water star 8 changes location according to the period of the house. It also depends on the facing direction of the house. Once you have determined its location however, activating it correctly will enable your money luck to take root and blossom.

T here are several factors to take account of when activating the flying water star 8 in any building. Those who live on landed property and who have a garden would benefit from activating the flying water star 8 outside in their garden with a significant water feature, preferably one that is deep and filled with clean, clear water.

They can simultaneously activate the flying water star 8 inside the home itself, and for those who are greedy (like me) they can also activate in all the public rooms of their home. Living rooms and dining rooms, as well as TV rooms and family rooms, benefit from having the **flying water star 8 corner** activated with water. Those living in apartments have no choice but to activate the flying water star 8 inside their homes. For them, if the flying water star 8 is located in a patio or balcony that has a big picture window view, the flying water star 8 takes on increased potency.

In the same way, if the flying water star 8 sector corresponds

to the front of the house, either because it is located in the facing palace or on either side of the facing palace, it would be doubly auspicious. Just make sure that in building a water feature you do not inadvertently place it on the right hand side of the main door (inside looking out). Water on the right of the main door can cause the husband to develop a roving eye!

Activating the flying water star 8 for the whole house and in individual rooms in the house activates the big as well as small tai chi of homes. I have discovered that activating the small tai chi is sometimes good enough to improve one's income levels. But it is important also to ensure that bedrooms, kitchens and storerooms are left well alone. In these rooms, water can often create problems, so it is best to focus your attention to the garden and the living and dining rooms of house interiors when it comes to water.

This yang water feature with water lilies is an effective water star enhancer outside the house.

Swimming Pools

Swimming pools are great for activating money luck. Besides lending great aesthetic value to the home, these large water features can be powerful wealth enhancers. But pools must be located correctly and to be effective there are important guidelines to take note of. Here are some **swimming pool basics** that are useful to remember if you are thinking of adding a swimming pool to your garden, especially if you are doing it for feng shui reasons.

Check that the location where you plan to locate the pool or pond will definitely bring financial luck to the house. Here are some ground rules to follow:

1 Pools are usually dug into the ground, so you MUST make sure the location selected does not have an auspicious mountain star in the flying star natal chart of your property. If an auspicious mountain star inadvertently "falls" into a hole/water, it can bring enormous loss to the family.

2 It does not matter what shape your pond or pool is, but a regular shape is always better than an irregular shape, and a curved pool is to be preferred to one with sharp corners that can create poison arrows.

3. If you have "fountains" and jacuzzi type spouts that spray water into the pool, make sure that the water is being sprayed inwards and not outwards.

4. Pools should best occupy the sector that has the flying water star 8. This is regarded as the most auspicious location for the pond or pool. But swimming pools can also be auspicious when placed in the North, East and Southeast, based on the theory of the five elements.

5. If your house is changed into a Period of 8 house, then placing a pool or pond in the Southwest is also very beneficial. This taps what is known as the **indirect spirit** of the property. Take the direction from the center of the property. Activating the **indirect spirit** of the home with water is said to be very lucky.

6. A pool is always better when it is located at the front of the house rather than behind the house. However, if the water star 8 is in a back sector, as shown in this Period 8 house on the right, then placing the pool there is beneficial. Do note that in many of the Period 8 charts, you will find the "double 8" stars where both the mountain and water stars 8 occur in the same sector. In such instances, you will have to decide whether you wish to activate the water or mountain star 8. In the example of the house shown here, its whole layout and arrangement suggests that it is sensible to have a pool at the back of the house (as shown here). A rectangular pool here makes it a **wood** element shape. Since it is located in the South, a fire energy location, the shape of the pool here is harmonious to its sector.

7. Whenever you build a pool for feng shui reasons, it is vital that there is an opening into the house nearby, such as a door or a large window. This ensures that the good wealth Chi created can enter the house. If the pool faces a wall, the Chi created is lost.

Finally, it is necessary to ensure that the pool is kept scrupulously clean and moving at all times. Never allow large pools of water to get stagnant, or worse, to become dirty. And if for some reason you have decided not to maintain the swimming pool, it is VITAL

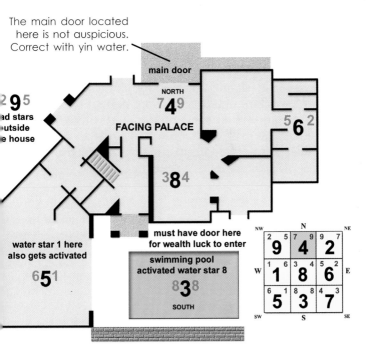

The main door located here is not auspicious. Correct with yin water.

main door

NORTH
7 **4** 9

FACING PALACE

2 **9** 5
...d stars
...utside
...e house

5 **6** 2

3 **8** 4

must have door here for wealth luck to enter

water star 1 here also gets activated

6 **5** 1

swimming pool activated water star 8

8 **3** 8

SOUTH

NW	N	NE
2 ⁵ 7 9 9 ⁷		
9	**4**	**2**
1 ⁶ 3 4 5 ²		
1	**8**	**6**
6 ¹ 8 8 4 ³		
5	**3**	**7**

W ... E
SW ... S ... SE

House facing NORTH 2/3

that you close up the pool. It is bad feng shui if a pool is left as a dry hole in the ground with no water. It is equally bad if water is allowed to get dirty with lack of maintenance. Either is sufficient to send your luck on a downward spiral.

Flow of Water

If you are able to build an artificial waterfall bringing a flow of auspicious water towards your house, this is believed to be an amazingly powerful way of creating a flow of good fortune riches to your home, benefiting the entire family and all residents residing within, often including the maid and other employees as well. Building a waterfall suggests a **flow of water** and this is not the same as a **water feature**.

A water feature symbolises a **body of wealth**, while a flow suggests an **income stream**. The aim of having good feng shui is to ensure one's family wealth is protected and safeguarded, and that it swells and expands with the years. This kind of feng shui usually benefits from having a body of water such as a swimming pool. A flow of water suggests a continuous inflow of income, and this usually suggests a good steady flow of profits or a good steady income in the form of salary.

When building a flow of water around your home, it is important to ensure the flow is inwards and that its flow pass your main door is auspicious. So if you build a waterfall in your garden, you should make sure the water passes your front door correctly and that it does not visibly flow away from your house.

So a waterfall is a **water flow feature** and is different from a pool or a pond.

Note however that when there is a "flow of water" in, or near, or around your property, or if you decide to build an artificial

waterfall, it is advisable to consult the *Yellow Emperor Classic* on auspicious water flows rather than the Flying Star formula.

Water flows can bring great good fortune indeed, but it can be very difficult to build the

direction of flow correctly. I have seen many instances where building the **water dragon** in the garden based on the water formulas have been fraught with difficulties.

So I would advise anyone wanting to build a waterfall in their compound to do so with care. Having said that however, when there is an artificial waterfall in your compound and it ends in a pond at the precise spot where there is a water star 8, then the good fortune is truly quite enormous and special.

If you decide to use a waterfall to enhance your wealth sectors, ensure the water flows towards the house and not away from it.

ENSURE THAT THE FLOW OF WATER PASS YOUR MAIN DOOR IS AUSPICIOUS

When the main door faces a cardinal direction i.e. NORTH, SOUTH, EAST or WEST, make sure water flows pass the main door from **left to right**.

When the main door faces NORTHWEST, SOUTHWEST, SOUTH EAST or NORTHEAST, make sure water flows pass the main door from **right to left**.

Decorative Ponds

From a feng shui perspective, perhaps the most efficient enhancers of wealth luck is to create a decorative pond in a corner of your garden which corresponds to the place of the water star 8. These ponds usually work best when they are neither too small nor too large, and when they are filled with robustly growing water plants or stocked with hardy garden fish such as colourful guppies or better yet, the auspicious gold fish.

If you keep carp or other more predatory fish, you will not be able to keep plants in your pond as the fish will devour them. So it is up to you to decide what kind of water feature you want. It is a good idea to have a variety of water features outside in the garden. Invest in a small pump to keep water from stagnating, and also to fill the water with oxygen making it healthier for your fish. If you like, you can grow water lilies or lotuses, as these symbolise purity. The lotus is also an especially auspicious flower. Each time it blooms, it attracts very good relationship Chi.

Terrapin or tortoise ponds are exceptionally auspicious when located in the North. This direction will have its protective Chi activated when there are images or symbols of tortoises. This celestial creature is very powerful and the real thing is always the best, since it is alive and thus already has a large store of *yang* energy.

Water lily ponds are decorative and effective water features. Always keep the water clean.

Natural Rivers And Lakes

 If you are fortunate enough to live on land that faces a natural pool of water such as an old mining pond or a natural lake, you really should make an effort to orientate your house to take advantage of the natural water near you. Similarly if you live by a slow flowing river. Treat these natural bodies of water as a start to designing the feng shui of your house. You can use the flying star natal chart to map out a facing direction for your house that will best allow you to "tap" into the water.

S tudy the Period 8 charts that apply to your home carefully before making any renovations to change it to a Period 8 house. If you are building a new house, it will be easier, as you can design your house to tap any favourable orientation that allows you to "capture" the wealth Chi of the water near you. There is more flexibility.

It does not matter whether the lake or pond is in front of you or behind you or by the side. As long as you use a compass to determine its location *vis a vis* your house, you can determine if there is a flying star chart that has the water star 8 in the direction of the lake.

If there is a chart that suits your house orientation and that enables you to capture the water Chi from the lake, you should ensure that your orientation is fine-tuned to take advantage of the water.

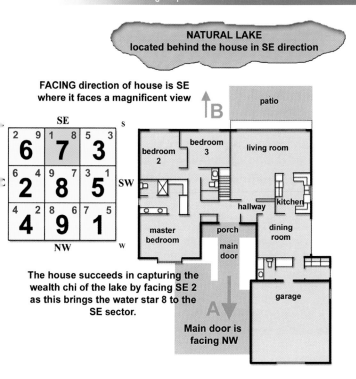

NATURAL LAKE
located behind the house in SE direction

FACING direction of house is SE where it faces a magnificent view

The house succeeds in capturing the wealth chi of the lake by facing SE 2 as this brings the water star 8 to the SE sector.

Main door is facing NW

This means that if the facing direction of the house is Southeast, as shown in the example above, you must make sure your house is facing SE 2, the second sub-direction, rather than SE 1, since this is what brings the water star 8 to the Southeast sector. Do be reminded that in Flying Star feng shui, it is the facing direction of the house and not the main door that determines the flying star natal chart.

Capturing The Chi of A River

The feng shui texts on landscapes, mountains and rivers always advise that if your home is built near a river, successfully tapping into the Chi of the river will be most auspicious. The texts always suggest that the river (or water) should "embrace the house". In addition, a natural waterway that flows pass the front of the house is said to be preferred to waterways that flow pass the back, since the latter suggests missed opportunities.

It is always best to have a river flow pass the front of the house. But there must also be an opening - a door or a window - that faces the river. Only then will favourable Chi that flows by enter the home. The window or door should be kept opened at least for part of the day. It is also a good idea to use the Period 8 flying star charts to determine whether

your house has the opportunity of tapping into the wealth Chi of the passing river. In the example here, we have a NE 1 facing house and the Period 8 chart shows that the water star 8 is in front. So the river is most auspicious. Also the river flows from right to left and since the facing direction of the door is Northeast, this too is favourable.

Note that if this house faces NE 2/3, the water star 8 will be at the back of the house and the mountain star 8 would be in the front. In such a situation, the river brings misfortune, as the auspicious mountain star 8 would have "fallen" into the river.

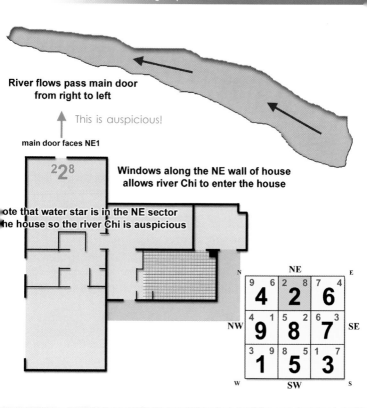

River flows pass main door from right to left

This is auspicious!

main door faces NE1

22 8

Windows along the NE wall of house allows river Chi to enter the house

ote that water star is in the NE sector
he house so the river Chi is auspicious

NE		
9 6 **4**	2 8 **2**	7 4 **6**
4 1 **9**	5 2 **8**	6 3 **7**
3 9 **1**	8 5 **5**	1 7 **3**

So note how vital it is to fine-tune the facing direction, as this is what determines the chart, and by extension, the location of the auspicious water star 8.

223

Man Made Waterfalls

Here is an example of how you can use a flying star chart to locate a small waterfall in your garden, with a view to enhancing wealth luck for the home. The chart here is a Period 8 chart of a house that faces the direction East 1. In this chart, the facing palace benefits from the auspicious double 8, so at the front of the house, both the water and mountain stars are auspicious. Since it is the front of the house, I would prefer to activate wealth luck using water, and because I do not wish to spoil the mountain star 8 in the process, I recommend building a waterfall instead of digging a pond.

So please note that when you have the double 8 in your chart, the way to "activate" both the lucky mountain and water stars in the chart would be to build a small waterfall.

Do this at the back or front of the house in accordance to whether the double 8 is in the facing or sitting palace. Using a waterfall will create the symbolism necessary to suggest both a mountain image as well as a water presence. Remember that by cleverly activating the double 8 chart this way brings enormous good fortune to the household. There are other Period 8 charts that also have this double 8 phenomenon, so do look out for them.

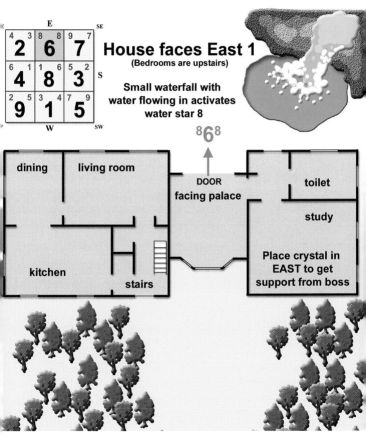

E		SE
4 3 **2**	8 8 **6**	9 7 **7**
6 1 **4**	1 6 **8**	5 2 **3** S
2 5 **9**	3 4 **1**	7 9 **5**
W		SW

House faces East 1
(Bedrooms are upstairs)

Small waterfall with water flowing in activates water star 8

8**6**8

↑

DOOR
facing palace

dining

living room

toilet

study

Place crystal in EAST to get support from boss

kitchen

stairs

Double 8 In The Sitting Palace

Here is an example of a double 8 mountain and water star flying into the back of the house, so that it is placed in the sitting palace. This is a Period 8 chart of a house that faces the direction South 1.

The chart is shown superimposed onto the house whose wealth luck benefits from the pond at the back of the house. But this same pond "kills" the auspicious mountain star 8 placed there. Residents in this house thus enjoy good money luck BUT the relationship and health luck of the residents is negatively affected. This is because the auspicious mountain star 8 is said to have fallen into the pond. If there had been an artificial waterfall built at the back instead of a pond, then both the auspicious mountain and water star 8 would benefit. One way to activate the mountain star here is to create an artificial "mountain" (a wall for instance) at the back. Note there should be a door or window to benefit from water and mountain stars luck. At the same time, the 9/7 stars in the facing palace must be corrected by having a small urn of yin water placed strategically here.

226

This house requires yin water here to correct the 9/7 stars in this sector. Otherwise there is danger of burglaries.

Facing South 1

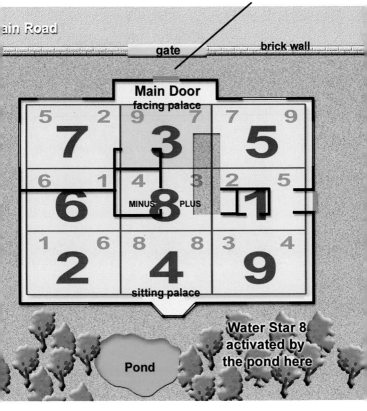

227

Water 8 With Mountain 5

Here is an example of a chart where the water star is the auspicious 8 and the mountain star is the unlucky misfortune star 5 in the sitting palace at the back of the house. Here it would benefit to build a swimming pool or a fishpond at the back of the house as shown in the diagram. This would mean digging a hole in the ground, which thus enhances water, while killing the mountain.

Note that the facing direction of this house is deemed to be the direction that faces the road and the view of the city beyond. The flying star chart is therefore drawn according to the direction SW 1, even though the main entrance into the house is facing NE 1. In this example, you can see how the correct selection of the facing direction of a house is so vital. In this case, the family will almost always enjoy the house while sitting in the patio, taking in the city view.

Placing a swimming pool in the back of the house overlooking the city thus enhances the feng shui of this house very significantly.

MAIN ROAD   **VIEW OF CITY BEYOND**

Facing direction is SW 1

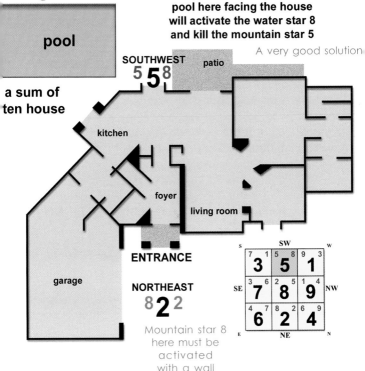

pool here facing the house
will activate the water star 8
and kill the mountain star 5

A very good solution

pool

SOUTHWEST   patio
5 **5** 8

**a sum of
ten house**

kitchen

foyer

living room

ENTRANCE

garage

NORTHEAST
8 **2** 2

Mountain star 8
here must be
activated
with a wall

	SW	
7 1 **3**	5 8 **5**	9 3 **1**
3 6 **7**	2 5 **8**	1 4 **9**
4 7 **6**	8 2 **2**	6 9 **4**

S — SW — W / SE — NW / E — NE — N

NOTE
In this house the facing direction is behind
the house which faces city view and road.

229

Water Inside The House

In the practice of feng shui, you can be as greedy as you wish, so having activated good **water Chi** in the environment surrounding the home, you can next turn your attention to activating water **inside** the house. Placing decorative water in the interiors of dwelling places is very much a modern day phenomenon. In the old days, water activation in feng shui was generally an outdoor matter. Modern day living, however, has seen individual homes evolve into beautiful and comfortable sanctuaries.

Young upwardly mobile couples are today getting increasingly house-proud. The art of designing private abodes has become a very important aspect of modern 21st century living. People have acquired the "nesting instinct" and to own one's own home has become a vital part of people's aspirations. The challenge lies in designing cozy, warm homes that have good energy. Not only will such homes bring good fortune, the residents also "feel" good inside their homes. One of the best ways to achieve this is with the soothing sound of moving water.

In this house, the small pond outside, in front of the main door, activates the water star 8, thereby benefiting the home. In the interiors, in applying the small tai chi, note how we have demarcated the dining room

and living room as separate entities. So the water star 8 which is in the West is deemed to be in the West part of the living room when we activate it in the living room, and in the West part of the dining room when we are activating the dining room. This then is the way to activate the water star 8 in each separate room inside the house. We are applying the principle of **small tai chi**.

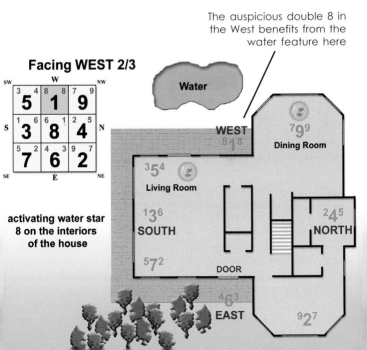

The auspicious double 8 in the West benefits from the water feature here

Facing WEST 2/3

SW	W	NW
3 4	8 8	7 9
5	**1**	**9**
1 6	6 1	2 5
3	**8**	**4**
5 2	4 3	9 7
7	**6**	**2**
SE	E	NE

S ... N

activating water star 8 on the interiors of the house

Water

WEST
8 1 8

⁷9⁹
Dining Room

³5⁴
Living Room

¹3⁶
SOUTH

²4⁵
NORTH

⁵7²

DOOR

⁴6³
EAST

⁹2⁷

Water Features For The Home

Water features for the home can be in the living areas such as courtyards or dining rooms. They can be made more **yang** with cleverly selected water plants. In recent years, so many beautiful water plants have been developed and domesticated for indoor use that one is simply spoilt for choice. With a little creativity, it is possible to create the most amazingly beautiful water garden in a private corner of the living or dining rooms of homes. Add in the feng shui dimension by making certain that the corner you select to place the "water garden" is also auspicious and you would have done something to improve your wealth luck. It is that easy!

There is something magical about water. Its presence cools down a warm room, and it emanates a soothing ambience to any environment. So water features are exceptionally efficient at creating a relaxing feeling inside homes. In addition, as we have seen, one can add the feng shui dimension simply by identifying the corner that houses the water star 8, and then designing a water feature to place in that corner. Do this by superimposing the natal chart of the house, or apartment building, onto the room to be decorated.

When you do this, you are applying the **small tai chi** principle, and it works beautifully in identifying the corner of the living room that houses the auspicious water star 8. You can ask your interior designer to then create a room or internal courtyard around the

Water inside the house can be an aquarium or a small fishpond placed in a courtyard adjacent to the living room. It can be a simple wide-rimmed pot filled with water and auspicious plants, such as free flowering lavender coloured hyacinths shown here. You can dress up the water feature with auspicious goldfish. Goldfish can be the real thing OR a cleverly faked piece, as shown in this water feature that adorns a small internal landscaped courtyard.

water feature being part of a certain corner. If you prefer, you can use a water feature which has a rotating crystal ball placed above a small bowl of moving water. This is especially good for those in business because an actively rotating crystal ball symbolises never-ending turnover, which is good for increasing sales income.

Water always has greater feng shui significance when combined with auspicious symbols, thus complementing with auspicious symbols of good fortune such as fish or celestial creatures such as tortoises and three-legged toads is always a good idea.

The symbols you use can be the real thing or they can be man-made. Remember that feng shui is totally symbolic – all objects, real or inanimate, has Chi energy, so the choice is yours. I use both real, as well as man-made symbols. Pictured on the left above is a very effective water feature using an ingot and rolling ball to simulate continuous good turnover. At home, I keep pet terrapins who have been with me for a long time indeed.

Their names are Drew, Dylan and Dickson - they have brought me good fortune now for many years and they live in the auspicious water sector in the North sector of my home which also corresponds to the place of the auspicious water star 8.

There are many different kinds of water features that are freely available these days, many of them inexpensive and often cleverly adorned with crystal carps, dragons, three-legged toads, tortoises and so forth. These traditional good fortune symbols add great depth and beauty to the lucky Chi created. Indeed, my favourite feng shui tip which I share with many friends is that there should be a dragon next to any water feature, since this really does make such a vital difference. Water features that are accompanied with dragon images symbolise the thirsty dragon "getting water" and this has always been a very powerful way of energising for good fortune luck. If you already have a water feature in your house, first check that it has been placed in the correct corner, and then make certain you place a dragon next to it.

The Taoists are great believers in using the dragon image this way. Look for a golden dragon that appeals to you, and place it near your water feature. For a long time this was the "secret" which Taoist feng shui masters kept very much to themselves.

Creative Water Features

You really can be as creative as you wish when it comes to designing water features to enhance the feng shui of your home or any office building. The important thing to remember is to make certain the water is located correctly according to flying star charts, since this does have an enormous impact on your money luck. Also, never forget to take note of other **taboos** with respect to the placement and use of water – please remember that when using feng shui recommendations from one school or method, it is important to check that you are not breaking an important taboo based on another method of feng shui. When decision-making becomes difficult, use a trial and error approach. Monitor the effect of any new water feature for at least three months. And then be as creative as you wish!

Here is a picture of a very creative and spectacular water feature placed at the entrance to Downtown Disney in Anaheim, California. This is a relatively recent development, which was opened last year, and I was told that a feng shui consultant was brought in to design the placement of this waterfall. Please note that this kind of waterfall does not represent water flowing out, as there is a pool just below the waterfall to symbolically catch the water. Downtown Disney is a very busy tourist attraction and on my recent visit there in

June 2003, I could see that the energy was very *yang* and definitely very auspicious. There were so many attractive water features incorporated into the design of this fabulous township, it did not surprise me that almost every retail shop and restaurant here seemed to be doing very well indeed.

Despite the much-publicised downturn in the economy, as well as the much-reduced number of people traveling, Downtown Disney was nevertheless very well patronised indeed.

Activating Mountain Stars For Relationship Luck

The Mountain Stars

The mountain stars of the Flying Star system of feng shui govern all aspects of relationship and health luck. When you live in a room that is visited by an auspicious mountain star, you will benefit hugely from excellent relationship and health luck. Luck manifests in the way people react to you - with warmth, support and goodwill. You will find it easy to make friends, be well liked and generally be made to feel that the world is a very agreeable place indeed. When you activate an auspicious mountain star with the correct placement of mountain symbols, your relationships will become the source of extreme good fortune, and you will enjoy reasonably good health as well. So never forget to pay equal attention to the mountain star 8.

Many of the feng shui masters from Hong Kong are fond of recommending mountain landscape paintings as part of their practice.

When I worked in Hong Kong many years ago, one of the things that struck me each time I visited the offices of any of the senior Chinese bankers there was that many of them had beautiful mountain paintings hanging in certain corners of their visitors rooms, as well as inside their private offices.

A Taoist master explained to me that mountains were not only powerful symbols of

support; they also signified the essence of the celestial dragon. It was then that I was introduced to the concept of **mountain stars** - the sitting stars or **chor sin** of feng shui terminology. "When you activate the lucky mountain stars correctly," I was told, "your family and descendants luck will be most superior. You will enjoy good health, live to a ripe old age and be able to enjoy your children and your grandchildren."

Often, just hanging the painting of a beautiful mountain scene where an auspicious mountain star resides is sufficient to activate its benevolent effects. When you use such a picture, however, you must make sure the mountain is one you feel good affinity with.

Auspicious Mountain Stars

When you have mastered the art of selecting the correct flying star chart that applies to your house, you will also have learnt to locate the place of the relationship luck sectors in and around your house and office.

The mountain star is what symbolises everything to do with relationship, health and descendents luck of the residents.

When the mountain star number is lucky, it brings wonderful relationship luck not only to the sector it occupies, but also to the entire household when it is correctly activated. And when it is an unlucky or afflicted number, it will likewise bring loss of popularity and problems in relationships with loved ones, and this will often be followed by sickness and ill health as well. The mountain star is thus very important.

If a **good** mountain star is in the North

If the mountain star 8 is in the North, note that placing a mountain image here, especially one that is of the Earth element, would clash with the element of the North, which is water – as Earth overcomes Water. This would seem to flout conventional feng shui wisdom, since the presence of Earth in the North is said to affect one's career luck under the Pa Kua Eight Aspirations system of feng shui. So when the mountain star 8 flies to the North, it can present a real dilemma.

For expert masters of feng shui, however, this is not a problem, since their in depth knowledge of the five elements goes beyond

Natural quartz crystal clusters make excellent mountain star 8 energizers. These are the most powerful of activators.

the usual superficial interpretation of the cycle of the five elements. According to them, when the flying mountain star 8 enters the North, it presents a good opportunity for the elements Earth and Water to combine effectively, thereby producing an environment that is conducive for plants to grow and flourish. This signifies luck that creates the formation of strategic alliances - in business as well as in marriage opportunities - for the children of the family.

To tap into this kind of luck, the placement of special crystal formations that signify the **treasures of the earth** would be most effective. What is needed is a strong cluster of natural crystals. Placing a small light embedded inside the crystal cluster will activate it.

If a **bad** mountain star is in the North, East or Southeast

When an unlucky mountain star flies into any one of these three directions - North, East or Southeast - these sectors will benefit residents hugely when there is the presence of water. The best way to overcome or control any bad mountain star, while simultaneously activating the water element, would be to dig a hole in the ground and fill it with water.

This means creating a small decorative pond or even having a pool here. This is because the best way to control a bad mountain star – a bad mountain star destroys all your relationships and plays havoc with your love life – is to symbolically dig a hole in the ground. This then activates the symbolism of the **mountain falling into the water** cure.

The picture shown here aptly symbolises this powerful flying star cure. According to many feng shui masters, usually just a hole in the ground can symbolise water. Thus, whenever you feel the bad effects of a negative mountain star (e.g. when the numbers are 2 or 5), the best antidote is to create some kind of hole in the ground.

While on the subject of digging a hole, please note that generally speaking, it is never advisable to dig a hole inside the home if you are renovating a home. The time to have a pond inside the home is when the house is being built, not during times of renovations. The only way to create a pond inside the home is to build around an existing pond that is outside the home. This way, the feng shui of both the home as well as the pond will be at its maximum best. Digging a hole inside your home usually suggests a loss of wealth.

It is also not a good idea to use the water cure to overcome bad mountain stars that fly into bedrooms. Water, and worse, any kind of pond inside the bedroom is extremely harmful. Inside the bedroom, the best way to control an unlucky mountain star is to use the five element theory. Thus hanging windchimes would be the best cure. Using this method, we will then be attempting to directly exhaust the earth numbers 2 and 5. If you use windchimes as a cure, make sure they are all metallic with 6 rods, and that they are hung by the sides of the rooms. Do not sleep, walk or sit directly under any windchime.

Mountain Star Eight

During the Period of 8, the luck of this number is incredibly special. You should look for the mountain star 8 in your natal chart to activate your relationship and health luck. When you find it, make an effort to energise it with a suitable **mountain** symbol.

Check if the lucky mountain star 8 has "flown" into any of the following important rooms of the house.

1. The facing palace of the house - i.e. the foyer of the house where the main door opens. If the mountain star 8 is located here, then placing crystal balls, natural crystal clusters or crystal products here would activate the mountain star 8 bringing wonderful relationship luck.

2. The master bedroom. Here, the mountain star 8 benefits the most important people in the house and it is best activated with an amethyst crystal cluster or a natural quartz crystal cluster. Place these under the foot of the bed.

Activate a mountain star 8 in the bedroom with an amethyst crystal cluster.

3. The sitting palace of the house - i.e. the back of the house, which symbolises where the house sits. Usually, when the mountain star 8 is behind the house, it is beneficial to have a small hill slope at the back or to have a solid wall there to signify the mountain. The granite stone wall shown below emphasises Earth energy, and this is excellent if the mountain star in this corner of the house is auspicious. Also note the natural slope of the land. When the back of the house has a slope like this, it is beneficial when the mountain stars in the back sectors of the house are lucky numbers, since the slope acts as a natural energiser.

Activating Mountain Star 8

One of the most important ways of ensuring that your family enjoys good health and relationship luck is to energise the sector occupied by the **flying mountain star 8**. Finding its location in your house depends on your house period as well as its "facing direction". This gives you the flying star natal chart of your house. Once you have determined the location of the lucky mountain star, activating it correctly will bring you wonderful relationship luck that leads to much love and happiness.

T here are several factors to take account of when activating the **mountain star 8** in any building. Those who live on landed property and who have extra land would benefit from activating the flying mountain star 8 outside in their garden with a significant wall feature, preferably one that is high enough and clearly seen as a special feature of that part of the house. They can simultaneously activate the flying mountain star 8 inside the home itself - in all the most important rooms of the home where the family gather, such as the family room, TV room and dining room.

Such rooms benefit hugely from having the **flying mountain star 8 corner** activated with a mountain symbol. In the example of a SW 1 facing house shown here, these corners are marked as red squares.

Those living in apartments have no choice but to activate the flying mountain star 8 inside their homes. For them, if the

flying mountain star 8 is located in a patio or balcony that has a big picture window view, and there is a view of mountains in the distance, the flying mountain star 8 takes on increased potency.

In the same way, if the flying mountain star 8 sector corresponds to the back of the house, either because it is located in the sitting palace or on either side of the sitting palace, it is good feng shui to build a wall in that part of the back. Once again, you can see that in practical feng shui, you can use the small tai chi concept to activate inside as well as outside the home.

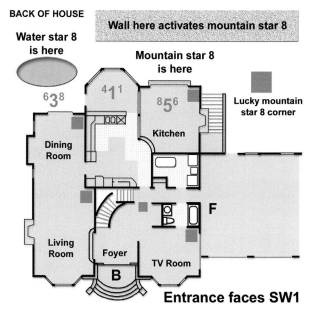

BACK OF HOUSE

Wall here activates mountain star 8

Water star 8 is here

Mountain star 8 is here

6 3 8

4 1 1

8 5 6

Lucky mountain star 8 corner

Dining Room

Kitchen

Living Room

Foyer

F

TV Room

B

Entrance faces SW1

249

Decorative Walls

Decorative walls offer scope for designers to bring great aesthetic value to the practice of feng shui. There is no limit to the versatility of walls, but for them to have any feng shui significance, they must be located correctly. Here are some basics that are useful to remember if you are seriously thinking of adding a decorative wall to your garden for feng shui reasons.

Check the location where you plan to locate the wall. If it sits exactly on where a lucky mountain star is located, the wall will definitely bring great friendship, social and even romance luck to the residents of the house. Here are some basic guidelines:

1. Walls are usually built above the ground, so you MUST make sure the location selected does not block the view of important doors. Shown in the picture on the facing page is a very solid wall made of marble, which would be an excellent mountain star activator if placed in the correct location. This wall feature is part of the overall concept of the famous Getty Museum in Los Angeles, USA, which I visited in June 2003.

2. Do take note that it does not matter how high your wall feature is, as long as it is never allowed to dominate the surrounding area. A mountain symbol must complement the house or building, creating support and pleasantly complementing the landscape. A wall feature built for feng shui reasons should never overwhelm its surroundings.

3. If you have "fountains" and jacuzzi type spouts that spray water into a pool that is adjacent to the wall, make certain the water is being spouted inwards and not outwards away from the house or building. It is not necessary to spoil your wealth luck while improving your relationship luck. Shown on the right is a very "mountain" dominated building design that also has a prominent water feature. Note here that the mountain dominates the shallow pool.

4. Feature walls best occupy the sector that has the flying mountain star 8, but they should never be positioned where the mountain stars 5 and 2 are located, as this would inadvertently activate these unlucky stars. Since 2 and 5 are Earth numbers, if you build a wall where these numbers are found, you would be activating their strength, causing misfortune to befall  the household. If you already have a wall built here where these numbers occur as mountain stars, simply grow a clinging vine to keep the earth element under control. This is shown in the picture above.

5. A wall is always better when it is located at the back of the house rather than in front of the house. However, if the mountain star 8 is in the front sector, then placing a decorative wall in the front is also beneficial. Do note that in many of the Period 8 charts, you will find the "double 8" stars where both the mountain and water stars 8 occur in the same sector, either at the back or at the front of the house or building. In such instances, you will have to decide whether you wish to activate the water star or the mountain star 8. You can do both of course, if you are clever about it.

For instance, you can build a decorative feature wall with a pool next to it, in a sector that has the double 8 mountain and water stars. When you resort to doing this, however, you will of course be taking the risk of having the auspicious mountain star "fall into the water". This depends on how deep the water is. Usually,

to make certain you do not waste a situation where the 8 water and mountain stars occur together, it is a good idea to activate the small tai chi of **both** the auspicious water and mountain stars inside the rooms of the building.

6. Finally, it is necessary to ensure that all your decorative walls are kept scrupulously clean and never overgrown with clinging vines unless you need the energy of the wall to be suppressed. Shown below is an excellent way of combining plants with walls without appearing to suppress the energy of the wall.

This imposing mountain feature was built in a corner of the building that houses an auspicious mountain star. Here the wall is made even more aesthetically beautiful by the introduction of green plants, but the plants do not overwhelm the marble wall feature.

Mountain Paintings

In the practice of feng shui, you can be as "kiasu" as you wish, so if you wish to ensure that you do not lose out on the auspicious relationship and health star, you can hang paintings or pictures of mountains in the auspicious mountain star corners of every important room in the house. This means having a mountain painting in your living room, your study and of course your bedroom.

Mountain paintings are easy to find. And especially if you like Chinese landscape paintings, one truly is spoilt for choice. You will find that many of the business tycoons of Hong Kong, Taiwan and China continue to hang stunning landscape paintings inside their homes and offices. There is always some special meaning to the mountain landscape paintings they select or commission. For instance, mountain shapes, colours and even the number of peaks and gorges have important feng shui significance.

For our purpose, it is suffice to know that when you hang mountain paintings to activate the auspicious flying mountain star or to create the support of the tortoise behind you at work, it is best to choose paintings that do not have water features painted in. More auspicious would be the presence of birds flying and the presence of auspicious vegetation and trees such as the pine tree.

This painting of mountains was executed with feng shui in mind. Note the pine trees in the foreground, the distant snow capped mountains and the flock of flying birds. The presence of birds is always good feng shui. Any kind of bird is fine, and the more of them there are, the better!

A Mountain of Gold

Another way of activating the auspicious mountain star is to create a mountain of gold where the auspicious mountain star is located. This can be a pile of stones spray painted to look like gold, or it can be a painting of mountains with real gold leaf pasted onto the mountain.

Changing House Period

Having familiarised yourself with the Period 7 and 8 charts, you now need to decide whether or not you really want to change the period of your house, thereby transforming it into a Period 8 house. This will ensure that the energy of your home does not stagnate, as it surely must. In reality, I feel there is really no choice. This is because in Flying Star feng shui, as soon as the 20 year period changes, all houses built or renovated in the period immediately preceding suffers from an instant dropping off of energy. It is as if the battery of the house has gone dead. Good luck starts to dissolve and recede.

D uring the period of 7, all houses built or renovated in period 6 lost energy and those who resided in such houses without changing its energy into period 7 suffered a decline in their fortunes. In the same way, all period 7 houses will lose energy as soon as the period changes to period 8 and the residents of such houses will start to feel a decline in their fortunes. Some feng shui masters contend that if your house was built and completed during the tail end of period 7, i.e. in 2002 or 2003, the house energy will continue to remain strong and even take on some of the energy of Period 8.

However, I am more inclined to go with the school of thought that insists that even a brand new house completed in 2003 MUST take specific measures to

transform its energy into that of period 8. This means a certain amount of renovation is needed. Having said this, however, there are some situations where the decision as to whether or not to change period is not so straightforward. These are addressed herewith.

What if the period 7 chart is better for your house?

A close investigation of the period charts for both period 7 and 8 does reveal that in many instances the period 7 chart does indicate a better distribution of luck than the period 8 chart. If this reflects your situation, it would seem that changing the period of your house will only bring you worse luck. My advice in such a situation would be to wait a year or two and see how the new period affects your luck. I have been told very strenuously that the quality of energy of any house based on its up-to-date period is usually far more important than the

map distribution of the luck. If this is indeed the case, then it would appear that even though the period 7 chart works better for you, you should still endeavour to change your house period, and then perhaps change its layout of rooms to conform with the new period 8 chart.

What if it my bedroom and main door gets hit by truly bad numbers under the Period 8 chart – do I still change?

The answer is yes, and it is beneficial to relocate the bedroom as well as the main door. Undertaking a renovation is always to effect a shift of energy, so re-designing the flow of Chi within the house can only be a good thing. Having said this, I understand that for many people, renovating their home is not an easy decision to make. Likewise, for me, I too have to change my house in the same way I did in the mid-eighties in order to safeguard my feng shui luck.

What if it is impossible for me to undertake any kind of renovations – e.g. I may be renting the house, or I cannot afford to undertake the renovations?

If it is impossible for you to undertake the renovations necessary to change your house period, one suggestion is to do the next best thing and that is to create an occasion for your house to be given a massive infusion of fresh new yang energy. Do this after the changeover date, i.e. 4th February 2004.

Here are several ways of creating massive yang energy for your house:

Firstly, organise a big house party after the changeover date. Invite as many people and friends as you can and make plenty of noise – it is important that the people you invite are positive people who have no hidden agendas in their friendship with you. You MUST ensure that the energy you create is positive and empowering – not negative and certainly not hostile. Make certain that you invite as many children as possible and hang lanterns, balloons and happiness symbols. Have a live band, make sure there is plenty of food and open all the doors and windows to allow fresh energy to infuse your home. A successful party with lots of happy smiling children is one of the best ways for rejuvenating stale and stagnated energy. The new energy should give you enough time to make the changeover a few years later.

Secondly, consider organising a lion dance. This is a very noisy and very effective way of creating "noise level". Most of the lion dance troupes in the Asian cities where they are popular are very familiar with the different types of lion dances. So tell them what you

want is a **Period Change** performance. In any case, having a lion dance during the lunar New Year is always auspicious. So if you really cannot change the period of your house, make sure you bring in the lions. Even if you can change your house period, it is a good idea to have the lions perform inside your house.

Thirdly, you can try giving your house a fresh coat of paint. A good way of creating fresh new energy would be to select a slightly louder colour than what you presently have. Also do note that the best colour for Period 8 is yellow – i.e. all shades of this earth colour. In the same way that white was a great colour for period 7 houses, so yellow is an extremely suitable colour for period 8. If you are not too adventurous with colours, select the lighter shades.

Nothing like a party to set yang Chi moving!

Changing Heaven Chi

There are three main things you need to do if you want to change your house into a Period of 8 house - the first of which is the need to change your heaven Chi. This means changing your roof.

T he feng shui masters of Hong Kong stress the great importance of changing the roof. "Unless you bring in fresh new energy from the heavens," they say, " how can the Chi of your house have been refreshed?"

To them, changing the roof is not merely a cosmetic job. It requires the old roof to be physically removed for at least three days, and for fresh roof tiles to then be put in its place.

For many, however, changing heaven Chi can be a symbolic activity. I believe that as long as the old roof is physically removed and new tiles put in its place, it is unnecessary to keep the house uncovered for as long as three days, especially if one is going through a rainy season. It is also not necessary to change the entire roof. As long as the roof over the main part of the house (the foyer area that corresponds to the facing palace) is changed, it should qualify. This allows fresh energy form the skies to flow through the house.

Finally, for those who want to save costs, it is not necessary for the entire roof to be changed into new tiles. As long as part of the roof has new tiles it should be sufficient. The rest of the tiles can be given a good wash and repainted.

Changing Earth Chi

The second change that has to be effected is to change the Earth luck of the house and this requires part of the floor to be removed and replaced with new floor. In modern homes, this suggests a change of floor tiles.

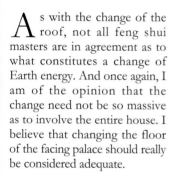

As with the change of the roof, not all feng shui masters are in agreement as to what constitutes a change of Earth energy. And once again, I am of the opinion that the change need not be so massive as to involve the entire house. I believe that changing the floor of the facing palace should really be considered adequate.

Also, if your renovations call for a new floor area to be created, then it is unnecessary to change any of the floor tiles of the existing house. Once there is addition of floor area, the house is said to have received an infusion of fresh new energy. This is an important clarification since changing floor tiles can be

a messy affair. In addition, it is also a good idea to give the house a completely fresh coat of paint. This is an important part of the exercise and there are feng shui experts who contend that a new coat of paint inside and outside the house is considered sufficient renovation to change the period.

I hesitate to agree on this matter, as I am a very *kiasu* sort of person. I prefer to make very certain that when I plan a renovation to change the period of my house, that I am doing enough to effect the change. Thus, while I will certainly advocate giving my period 7 house a fresh coat of new paint to change it to period 8, I will also change part of my flooring.

Changing The Main Door

The third thing to do is to change your main door. This is considered a cardinal requirement of a period change - unless the house gets a new main door, its energy is said to remain fixed in the old period.

C hanging the main door means a brand new door has to be made. If you are changing your house period, you might also want to use this opportunity to determine whether or not you wish to change the location of the front door. Since the main door determines the location of the facing palace, it stands to reason that one should select the front sector that has the "best star numbers" to locate the door.

Look at the example illustrated on the facing page. This is a house which faces West and enjoys the double 8 mountain and water star in the center front palace. In this case,

therefore, the front door should be moved from the left front sector into the middle front sector. It is useful to point out that in almost all the period 8 charts, the center sectors of the house enjoy the "best" luck. This suggests that in period 8, houses should be broad rather than narrow.

When a house is narrow and there are only two rooms occupying the width of a house, what happens, according to some flying star experts, is that the center grid of sectors literally disappears. This means that such houses cannot benefit from the auspicious number 8, which flies to the center grids of the house during the period 8.

264

I do not agree with this, as I see little merit this interpretation. Nevertheless, it is a good idea to symbolically create three distinct sectors to the width of the house, as this effectively captures the lucky 8 stars.

Another way is to have a whole room occupy the breadth of the house. This effectively "broadens" the center grids, thereby achieving the balance needed to tap the center grid numbers.

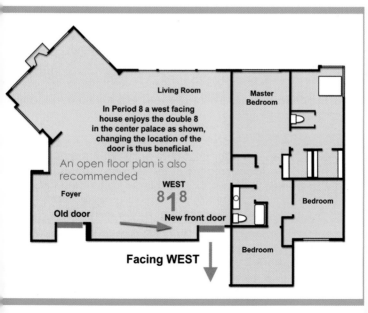

Taking Note of Annual Taboos

A very important thing to remember about renovations is that there are annual taboos that must be observed. These taboos are related to the afflictions of the annual flying star chart. There are three afflictions to take note of and these are the Grand Duke Jupiter or Tai Sui, the Three Killings (the **sarm saat**) and the Five Yellow (**wu wang**). It is important that we know where each of these afflictions is located in the year we plan on carrying out the renovation. This is because the sectors occupied by these three afflictions must not be disturbed. If they are, they cause serious bad luck to the residents.

Thus, starting from 2004, it is a good idea to find out exactly which sectors of your house cannot be disturbed. Here is a summary of the locations of these three afflictions.

IN 2004

You cannot renovate in the following sectors:
In Southwest 3, because the Grand Duke Jupiter resides there.
In the South, because the Three Killings resides there.
In the center, because the Five Yellow resides there.

IN 2005

You cannot renovate in the following sectors:
In West 2, because the Grand Duke Jupiter resides there.
In the East, because the Three Killings resides there.
In the Northwest, because the Five Yellow resides there.

IN 2 0 06

You cannot renovate in the following sectors:

In Northwest 1, because the Grand Duke Jupiter resides there.
In the North, because the Three Killings resides there.
In the West, because the Five Yellow resides there.

IN 2 0 07

You cannot renovate in the following sectors:

In Northwest 3, because the Grand Duke Jupiter resides there.
In the West, because the Three Killings resides there.
In the Northeast, because the Five Yellow resides there.

In each year, you should update your feng shui by checking the location of these annual afflictions. You can go online to **www.wofs.com** or you can check FENG SHUI WORLD magazine for regular updates. In the meanwhile, please note that the above taboos are especially significant if you are undertaking spot renovations. What is important is that these afflicted sectors must not be activated by banging, knocking, digging, cutting and so forth. When these afflictions are activated, they cause residents to suffer from loss, ill health and accidents.

If your renovations are going to be extensive, and you will be knocking, digging and banging all over the house, then you should simply ensure that your renovations do not START or END in any of the afflicted locations. Indeed, it is always beneficial to start and end renovations in sectors that enjoy auspicious annual and monthly flying stars.

Finally, when you undertake your renovations to change your house period, please ensure that you check the Feng Shui Almanac for the auspicious days and hours to begin work. Also, take note of which animal signs will be in conflict with the day that work begins. I suggest that you select a day that does not conflict with your animal sign or that of anyone living in the house.

267

Changing House Period